BRITAIN IN O

ORMSKIRK & DISTRICT

MONA DUGGAN

ALAN SUTTON PUBLISHING LIMITED

Alan Sutton Publishing Limited
Phoenix Mill · Far Thrupp · Stroud
Gloucestershire · GL5 2BU

First published 1995

Cover photographs: (front) The first car sold in Ormskirk; (back) Workmen building cottages for Lord Derby. *Title page photograph:* Fashions in nineteenth-century Ormskirk.

British Library Cataloguing in Publication Data.
A catalogue record for this book is available from the British Library.

ISBN 0-7509-0850-5

Typeset in 9/10 Sabon.
Typesetting and origination by
Alan Sutton Publishing Limited.
Printed in Great Britain by
WBC, Bridgend, Mid Glam.

The cottages and sawmill belonging to the Draper family in Parrs Lane, Aughton. One of their specialities was the construction of Dutch barns, many of which are still to be seen on the local farms. The steam engine which powered the saws was in the building at the back beneath the chimney at the right of the photograph.

Contents

	Introduction	5
1.	The Changing Townscape	7
2.	Sports and Leisure Activities	31
3.	Trades and Professions	43
4.	Special Occasions	77
5.	Young People	93
6.	From the Districts	115

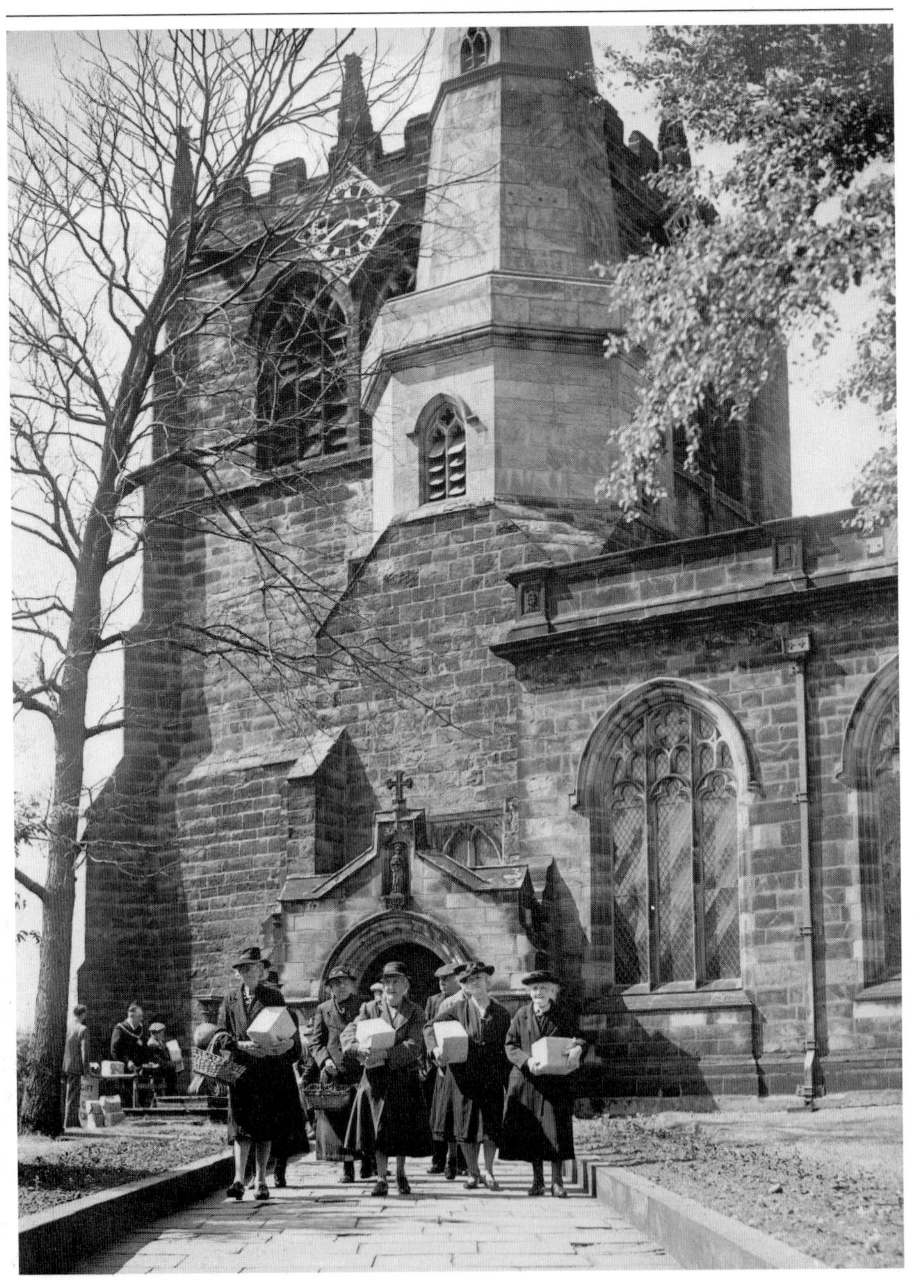

Old age pensioners leaving the church after a distribution of food parcels, 1949. The tower of Ormskirk Parish Church was constructed after the Reformation to house the bells of Burscough Priory, and the spire has been rebuilt several times on its old foundations. Ormskirk is one of the few English churches with both a tower and a steeple at the west end of the church.

Introduction

Most visitors to Ormskirk ask why the church has both a spire and a tower, and why they are both at the western end of the church. Sometimes they are told that the tower was built to house the bells of Burscough Priory after the Dissolution. At other times they are given the more fanciful answer that two benevolent sisters could not agree whether to endow the church with money for a spire or for a tower. Eventually they decided to fund the building of both.

Ormskirk is a town that prompts many questions. In its earliest history, the problem is the identity of Orm, who founded his church on the hill in the midst of the West Lancashire plain. Was he a Norse hermit, or an ancestor of the early lords of Lathom, or some kinsman of Uctred who owned much of the land hereabouts before the Conquest?

The principal question from the medieval period is why Ormskirk lost its status as a borough, granted to it in the thirteenth century at about the same time as it acquired its market charter. The pattern of land holdings along Aughton Street was, until recently, the pattern of the burgage plots granted to the burgesses of the ancient borough. When and why did Ormskirk revert to being a mere township?

For the Tudor period it is easier to answer the questions. The town grew in importance because the Earl of Derby was the lord of the manor of Ormskirk, and he was the son-in-law of Henry VII. The king with his court visited the town and worshipped in the church. Since that day, part of the chancel has been known as the King's Chancel. After that royal visit the fame of the town spread, its market prospered and it became a centre for glove-making and the leather trade.

In the seventeenth century the town experienced great poverty and hardship. Petitions were sent to the quarter sessions for help for the many destitute inhabitants. The main cause of this was the Civil War and, particularly, the battle for Lathom House. Hundreds of soldiers, many of them ill-fed and carrying disease, were stationed in the district. They foraged for food in the gardens, orchards and vegetable plots of the town and in the fields of the surrounding countryside. The inhabitants were left with little to eat and nothing to sell. Consequently, many fell ill and caught the plague, the market was closed until the danger of infection had passed, and many of the townsfolk were left with no means of earning a living.

Gradually, towards the end of the seventeenth century, the situation improved and all kinds of amenities were provided for visitors to the town. The race-course along what is now Long Lane in Aughton, the cockpit near the Mansion House and the spa in Lathom succeeded in attracting crowds to the town. Unfortunately, the boom did not last. Other towns in more accessible areas followed Ormskirk's lead in establishing similar attractions for the nobility and gentry, and Ormskirk's leisure amenities were abandoned.

The question from the nineteenth century is why the town did not develop into an industrial town. Many hand-loom silk weavers are recorded in the

Ormskirk censuses; it had a cotton factory, the leather industry continued to play an important role, coal was mined within three miles of the town, yet none of these industries grew to dominate its economy. One of the many answers to this problem was the state of public health locally in the middle years of the century. There was a large influx of Irish people fleeing the potato famine, and, as many of them were starving and had no resistance to disease, typhus and cholera spread rapidly among them. Also, sanitary conditions in the town were atrocious. The inhabitants appealed to the General Board of Health for help, and a local board was set up to initiate improvements. Bye-laws were passed to regulate street cleaning and the removal of refuse, conditions in the lodging houses were inspected and sewage schemes were completed, fresh water supplies were installed and, gradually, health returned to the town. Nevertheless, with a workforce debilitated by ill-health and poor living conditions, the town was unable to establish itself as a leading industrial centre and to meet the challenge of Wigan and other towns in south Lancashire not beset with such extensive difficulties. Instead, Ormskirk struggled to maintain its traditional role and to consolidate its marketing and service industries.

Thankfully, when we come to the early twentieth century, we have many means of investigating conditions in the town, and one of the most important is collections of contemporary photographs and personal experiences. They show us the town exactly as it was. The stallholders and shopkeepers with their wares and the costumes of the townsfolk give us a vivid impression of life in the recent past, while the memories of many of the inhabitants complete the picture.

Today the questions are why were so many of Ormskirk's old buildings pulled down in the twentieth century, why was the value of their architecture ignored, and why is Ormskirk's past never considered today when plans are drawn up for new roads, when streets and closes are named, or when precincts are planned? At the present there is great nostalgia for the past, a wish that Ormskirk had retained some of its old-world character as York, Shrewsbury and Ludlow have done. Unfortunately that has gone for ever, and many of these photographs record the demolition and desecration of relics of the old town. New developments are trying to recreate the old streets and courtyards, but are only succeeding in producing a planner's idea of an old-world town, not in recreating the original Ormskirk. There is a danger that all signs of the old town will be obliterated by demolition and re-siting, as occurred recently when Cockpit Lane was overlaid by the new town centre bypass. Perhaps this collection, kindly lent by so many good friends in Ormskirk, and the memories associated with the pictures, will succeed in curbing this passion for destroying the past, and will help to preserve some of the remaining roots of the town.

I must acknowledge the help and kindness extended to me in my search for these photographs, and the willingness of the people of Ormskirk and district to share their memories with me, and to lend me their precious mementoes of life in the early twentieth-century town. If there are mistakes in the captions, please forgive the lapses and wonder that so many clear memories still remain to describe Ormskirk and district in the early twentieth century.

Section One

THE CHANGING TOWNSCAPE

Burscough Street before the days of pedestrianization.

This sketch is an impression of Church Street, Ormskirk, at the end of the eighteenth century. In the foreground on the right-hand side of the cobbled street is the town hall, rebuilt in 1779. On the ground floor behind the arches was the meal-house where grain was sold on market days. At the back of this space were several butchers' shops, and above it was a large room used by the court leet, the quarter sessions and sometimes by the townspeople for assemblies or for the occasional visit of travelling players.

An Ormskirk photograph on a glass plate taken in the very early years of photography. It shows the Stretch family outside Vine House in Burscough Street. Their costumes suggest that the picture dates from the 1860s.

The market place, 1880s. The old, whitewashed King's Arms faces the clock tower and, on the right, a lady is buying fish at the fish stones. On the left-hand side of the road, gas lamps can be seen. The gas works were built in 1833, and Ormskirk was first lit by gas on 20 April 1835. Below, the same view after the rebuilding of the King's Arms, with the market in progress.

The magnificent frontage of the King's Arms when W. Tommas was proprietor. The black and white building next to the inn was the Corn Exchange, where crowds of the local farmers gathered on market days to discuss the price of grain, vegetables and livestock and, of course, to gossip.

The Corn Exchange. The glass veranda which sheltered generations of farmers was moved later to Burscough where it stood for many years in front of a shop. In Market Row, the narrow street alongside the Exchange, were the cottages of the local chimney-sweep and Jimmy Green, the barber.

The demolition of a row of old shops in Moor Street. In this picture the Midland Bank stands on the site of the Corn Exchange, and Market Row has been reduced to a narrow alleyway.

Further east on Moor Street, 1940s. The shops from left to right were Poole's printers, Taylor's stationers, Rimmer's pork butchers, Dowdle's wallpaper, and Wenk's florists.

Aughton Street, 1949. The Talbot Hotel, originally a coaching inn, can be seen on the right-hand side.

Stoker's furniture store on Moor Street – once the gas showroom. The Stoker family previously had a shop in Burscough Street where they sold millinery, drapery, clothes and furnishings.

Thomas's shop in Burscough Street next to a pub known as The Monkey's Nest – now Newlands DIY. Mrs Thomas sold baby linen and drapery in the left-hand side, while the rest of the shop was stocked with every kind of hardware and brushes.

The Institute on Moor Street, built in 1867. In this building dramatic and operatic societies staged their productions, and dances and other functions were held. The old building beside it was a shippon used by Tom Huston, whose wife sold vegetables in the yard.

The statue of Disraeli, unveiled by the Earl of Lathom in 1884, looks over the site after the Institute had been demolished. The land was used as a car park until the new bus station was built.

The Georgian building behind the statue of Disraeli, once the residence of the master of the workhouse, is now three shops. The house was used between 1860 and 1880 as a surgery by Dr Lax. Further down Chapel Street is the Mansion House, once the town house of the Stanleys of Moor Hall. Between 1841 and 1863 it housed the Mansion House Academy.

One side of a court off Chapel Street, the last remnant of the welter of courtyard developments built in Ormskirk during the nineteenth century. At that time sanitary provision was minimal, and conditions were atrocious in many of these courts.

The corner of Derby Street and Burscough Street. The corner house, once the home of the Heaton family, became the surgery of Dr Suffern and later Dr Temple. Earlier, the Misses Walker lived in the right-hand house in Burscough Street. They earned a living by making black puddings and sausages, and next door Miss Watson taught music. Below, the same site used for social services offices and for a car park.

A Georgian house lower down Burscough Street, recently known as Heartbreak House. This house was built in the late 1770s for Thomas Brandreth, who had a tannery at the back of this property. His son, Joseph, became a famous physician and moved to Liverpool, joining the staff of the infirmary there in 1780. In the early years of the twentieth century, the house became a school before being split up into bedsit accommodation. The cottage alongside the house was once a chapel, and later became the home of an ex-serviceman who had served for many years in the East. The house has now been renovated by a housing association. Further down the road were farm buildings where potato tubs were made, and where later Edward Jackson had his first saleroom.

Knowles House (left and above). William Knowles, vicar of Ormskirk from 1727 until 1780, built this house for his wife because, if he had died before her, the vicarage would have been transferred to the next vicar leaving her with nowhere to live. As it happened, she predeceased him and did not need the house after all. During the twentieth century it was the home of a succession of doctors, Dr Pendlebury and Dr Craig being the most recent. The archway led into a walled garden with cobblestone pathways. It was a beautiful house, as can be seen from the two small views of the interior taken shortly before its demolition to make way for the present library – a building which can only be described as utilitarian.

Thomas Stretch in the garden of Vine House, Burscough Street, with one of his famous pedigree collies.

These four pictures were taken in Burscough Street before the spate of demolition in the 1950s and its later pedestrianization. On the left-hand side is Bill Forshaw's butcher's shop, once Burgess's cycle shop.

Another Georgian house, known to local people as The Hall. Various doctors practised here, including Dr Marsden and Dr Sergeant. Further down the street the sign for the Wheat Sheaf Hotel can be seen.

A close-up of the Wheat Sheaf and Evans and Ball's provender merchants. In the 1930s, when two-way traffic was allowed in Burscough Street, Sentinel steam wagons from Kirkdale on their way to Preston docks used to mount the footway and touch the property on either side of the road.

At the bottom of Burscough Street. On the left are the old premises of Woolworth's – once Stoker's. On the right are Shepherd's grocers and the Maypole.

The Singer sewing machine shop in Burscough Street, 1929. Nora Hotchkiss and her elder sister are standing in the doorway.

Next door was Culshaw's tobacconists. The Culshaw family kept this shop for a hundred years. Edith Heyes (née Culshaw), pictured here, broke the long tradition when she retired in 1976.

The demolition of the Misses Ormeshers' tobacconist's shop next door to the White Lion in Church Street took place in 1958. Tragedy surrounded this building. The two sisters were murdered brutally in their home in Halsall Lane. The police never found the murderer and could find no motive other than robbery of the takings from this tiny shop. Then, when the building was being demolished, the ruins collapsed and a workman was buried. Fortunately he was rescued and survived the accident.

Church Street in the 1920s. Wood's the chemist's shop – later Boots – is on the left-hand side with a doorway on the corner. The handle on that door used to intrigue local children because it had been mended with a halfpenny.

The Parish Church with the path leading down to The Grove. Some of the cottages that lined this path can be seen to the left of the photograph.

The interior of the church during the late nineteenth-century alterations. The pillars, which had supported galleries above both the north and south aisles, are being replaced and the arcading with fluted pillars is being extended the whole length of the centre aisle.

A later view of the church. The new reredos of Russian oak is obliterating the lower part of the east window. The small balcony to the right of the east window has not been removed, nor has the sounding board over the pulpit been installed.

A view of Coronation Park, *c.* 1909. This was many years before the baths complex was built. The houses in The Grove had a clear view over the open parkland.

Bob Grayson (later Canon Grayson) with his mother and younger sister alongside the boating pool in the park, 1928.

Victoria Park on the corner of Ruff Lane and St Helens Road at the end of the nineteenth century. The photograph was taken before Abbeyfield and several of the other large houses were built and before the old cottages at the end of Ruff Lane had been demolished. Emmanuel Church can be seen in the background.

The old water tower at Scarth Hill. This has now been replaced by a mushroom-shaped construction which looks as if it has fallen from outer space.

An aerial view of the town taken from Tower Hill water tower. Greetby Hill School was built on the field in the centre of the photograph and opened in 1950. Bath Springs Brewery on the left has been converted into sheltered housing, and part of the field opposite Emmanuel Church has become the site of council offices. The field behind the cottages on Greetby Hill has been covered with houses and the open country visible between Railway Road and Burscough Street has been used for an industrial estate. Today the only open spaces in a view taken from this angle would be the playing fields around Greetby Hill School.

The Cottage Hospital on Hants Lane. The hospital was opened by the Countess of Derby on 22 January 1896 and this print was published by the *Ormskirk Advertiser* to commemorate the event. Later this hospital became known as the Brandreth Hospital. The Methodist Church can just be seen across open country on the left.

The Drill Hall was built in 1899 by public subscription on land donated by James Eastham, the brewer. It was used by the local territorials, the 2nd Lancashire Hussars, before being converted into the Civic Hall.

Two views of the market in progress on Moor Street. In front of the offices of Idle and Stretch, the third property from the right, is the weighbridge used for weighing coal carts.

Moor Street looking east during the Edwardian era, showing only one gabled building, the original Ship Inn, on the right-hand side. Later a similar frontage was added to the building next to it and the Ship Inn moved next door. Today the Ship sign can be seen on the left-hand building and a bunch of grapes on the original inn.

Section Two

SPORTS AND LEISURE ACTIVITIES

Ormskirk cricketers, 1898.

The Ormskirk 2nd cricket team, early 1920s. Back row, left to right: -?-, Tom Sharrock, Arthur Piggot, -?-, Doug Vickers, -?-, -?-, -?-, Umpire. Front row: -?-,W. Hulley, Charles Harrison, Walter Stretch, Gib Woods, -?-, -?-.

An Ormskirk cricket team, 1924/5. Back row, left to right: Umpire Jack Blease, Jack Draper, Jack Taylor, Frank Batty, Jack Price, Revd W. Ball, Umpire Ralph Grundy. Front row: Bert Ball, Ernie Talbot, Eddie Pearson, Gerald Ball, Harry Gore, Martin Molloy.

St Anne's cricket team, 1937. Back row, left to right: Frank Moran, Eddie Holcroft, Gillie Houghton, Frank Wills, Arthur Westby, Tom Moran, Joe Draper, Danny Murray. Middle row: Albert Moorcroft, Eddie Forshaw, Wilf Croft, Bert Ball, Tommy Colman, Tommy Latham. Front row: Jimmy Culshaw, Leo Wills, Johnnie Westhead, Joe Banks.

Walter Stretch batting on Ormskirk cricket field, 1920s. The notice on the railings is reputed to have read 'No Ladies or Dogs'!

Ormskirk Rugby Club, 1936. The occasion was the opening of the new ground between Halsall Lane and Asmall Lane. At this time, the Ormskirk side was remarkable because there were five brothers from the Lumby family all playing in the same team. Other local players included in the photograph are Harry Fry, Joe Schofield, Geoff Lewyer, Jack Heaton, Ken Lewis, Frank Oldfield and Jimmy Helm.

Balmoral Rugby Club on Castle Field, Westhead, in the early 1930s, when the captain was Fred Gibson. Seated left to right: Ralph Grundy, Jimmy Helm, -?-, Ronnie Brookes, Frank Oldfield. Among the other players are Eric Oldfield, Charles Burrows, Todger Tootall and two of the teachers from Aughton Street School, Sam Jowett and Eric Soar.

The Dray and Horses bowls team after winning the Lethbridge Cup, 1920s. Back row, left to right: -?-, Jack Wilding, George Webster, Jack Sumner, Micky Winrow, -?-, Harry Bell. Middle row: -?-, -?-, ?Winrow, -?-, Ernie Jackson, -?-, Bert Pennington. Front row: John Pennington, Charles Blackburn, -?-, George Thomley, Billy Waterhouse.

Ormskirk football team 1922–3. The men standing beside the team are, left to right, John Piers and Bert Ball and, at the other end, Harry Gore and Owen Wignall. The players included Paddy Davies, Charles Molloy, Jim Culshaw, John Molyneux, George Turner, Jack Robinson, Clarry Jones, Bill Fletcher and Fred Holt. They played on a field at the side of Hattersley's. The railway engine sheds can be seen in the background.

Cyclists' Club. In the early years of the twentieth century, many of the younger generation in Ormskirk joined cycling clubs. The town also became a venue for other cyclists, a welcome resting place on the way to Southport or to other more distant places. Several of the teashops, among them Burrow's of Church Street, catered for cyclists, and hung signs outside their shops to attract the visitors. Unfortunately, as this letter (right) testifies, not everyone welcomed the bikes – especially when they obstructed alleyways to joint properties.

TELEPHONE No. 6.

TELEGRAMS "DICKINSON, SOLICITOR, ORMSKIRK."

PARR, SADLER, DICKINSON & WATSON,

SOLICITORS.

AND AT SOUTHPORT.

FIRM { A. DICKINSON. W. H. WATSON.

Ormskirk, 11th May 1907

Dear Sir

Referring to your visit this morning and also to an interview we have had with Mr C Read we have to inform you that you have no right to use the covered passage and yard for storing Bicycles of customers visiting your premises.

Your rights are only a joint user of the covered passage to get to your house and the user of such part of the yard as may be necessary to enable you to enjoy the user of the privy and joint user of washhouse and ashpit.

Kindly let there be no further misunderstanding in this matter.

Yours faithfully

Parr Sadler Dickinson & Co

Mr Peter Burrows
Church Street

The Commercial Darts Team when they had won all three local trophies – the League Cup, the Clucas Shield and the Cooper Cup, late 1940s. Back row, left to right: Bruce Kitney, Harry Halliday, Sonnie Rice, Bob Woodcock, Joe Cheetham, Harry Hodge, Jimmy Hale. Front row: Bill Marsh, Eddie Sharples, Eric Skaife, Joe Webster, Eddie Birchall, Percy Caunce.

The top photograph opposite shows the Queen's Inn, Aughton Street, Darts Team, 1944–5. Holding the Clucas Shield is Joe Cheetham and on his right is Sonnie Rice. Among the other players are Bill Westhead and Andy Quinn.

Below is the Wheat Sheaf Darts Team when they had won both the Clucas Shield and the Cooper Cup, early 1950s. The lady enjoying the celebration is Amy Holland, manageress of the Wheat Sheaf. Among the players are Harry Marsden, Jim Melling and Frank Melia.

Ormskirk Operatic Society's production of *Tom Jones*, 1937. This society was started by members of Emmanuel Church, and the characters portrayed here are taken by Dick Renfrey, Olive Taylor and Arthur Bruce.

An early dramatic production which has proved impossible to identify. The setting suggests it took place at Church House and possibly the two male actors are Herbert Bate and Harold Jenkinson.

The Operatic Society's production of *The Gondoliers*, 1933.

Ormskirk Orchestra, before 1914. Joseph Taylor is the third clarinet at the back, while Milton Whittingham is on the bass drum.

The girls' training corps at the Empire Youth Parade, 1950. Their officer was Edith Robinson from Aughton, who had trained the girls to perform a morris dance – and had borrowed the equipment from the Belles of Aughton troop.

Norman Lea, as mascot of Ormskirk Town Band, 1934. Andrew Tolmey was the bandmaster at that time.

Section Three

TRADES AND PROFESSIONS

At work in Scott's slaughterhouse, Church Street.

Thomas Riding's workshop at the turn of the century. In 1854 Thomas Riding and J. Campbell started a joinery and building firm in Aughton Street. When they needed larger premises, they moved to Chapel Street where this workshop still stands, overshadowed by later development. The chimney for the steam engine which provided power for the saws and other machinery was pulled down many years ago, as was the Georgian townhouse alongside the factory yard.

RIDING & CAMPBELL,

JOINERS & BUILDERS,

&c.,

Bottom-end of Aughton Street,

ORMSKIRK.

PLANS AND SPECIFICATIONS
EXECUTED ON THE MOST REASONABLE TERMS.
ALTERATIONS AND REPAIRS PROMPTLY ATTENDED TO.

The buildings in the sketch opposite can be seen through the archway behind the group of workers employed by Thomas Riding during the early years of the twentieth century. Later the ornate walls, examples of the firm's high standard of craftsmanship, were altered and offices were built into them. Members of the Riding family in the photograph include William, his sons Thomas and Samuel, Mellor, the young man with the white apron, and Jack, the smallest boy sitting on the ground at the front of the group.

Riding's workmen building cottages for Lord Derby. Since medieval times the ancestors of Lord Derby provided housing for their tenants in the manor of Ormskirk.

Riding's men repairing the roof of the Parish Church. Mellor Riding can be seen next to the vicar near the parapet. They all seem oblivious to the height at which they are standing and to the magnificent view of the surrounding countryside.

Mellor Riding directing the bearers at the graveside during a military funeral. Another important part of Riding's business was undertaking.

Another firm of builders and joiners, Constantine's, 1902–3. This yard on Stanley Street is now the site of Ormskirk Glass. The man seated on the extreme left-hand side holding a clamp is Thomas Jones and the third workman at the back is Mr Banks.

Hattersley's brass foundry on Burscough Road before the extensions of 1939–40 were added. The firm was founded in 1897 by Richard Hattersley in his home town of Halifax. Then, after he had married Sarah Potter of Moor Hall in Aughton, he opened an office in Ormskirk. In 1916 this new factory was built among the fields on the outskirts of the town.

This small photograph dates from 1917 when Hattersley's was used as a munitions factory. Women had replaced the men, most of whom were serving in the forces. The mob-caps and overalls worn by the women show that even in those days the firm was safety-conscious. Such precautions were indeed necessary when machines were operated by a system of overhead line shafts, and when long hair and clothing often became entangled in the machinery with disastrous results.

Another section of the factory when the girls were producing munitions under the watchful eye of the charge hand, 1917. This room forms part of the factory complex today.

The canteen. Hattersley's were very progressive compared with many of their contemporaries, and provided cooked meals for their workers during wartime. The supervisors were segregated from the mass of factory floor workers and had their meals through the door marked 'charge hands'.

Church Street, ORMSKIRK, Apl 13th 1885

Mr Felleman

Bought of HOWARD & BALL,

Ironfounders & General Furnishing Ironmongers.

Agents for all kinds of Agricultural Implements, Oils, Paints, and Colours.

1 Hurricane Lamp 2/6

Paid with thanks
Pp John Ball

The premises of Howard and Ball, the iron founders and ironmongers on the left-hand side of Church Street. Their billboard can be seen in the centre of this view. At the other side of the street, beside the cyclists' alleyway, Burrow's confectioners and teashop – later Dorset's and now Swinton Insurance Agency – displayed a notice declaring that they had won the prize for gingerbread, the Ormskirk delicacy.

Sarah Woods, the original gingerbread lady. She baked the biscuits in a brick oven until they were fairly hard and would not crumble easily in her basket. For many years, Sarah sold her gingerbreads to passengers on the trains as they passed through Ormskirk station on the Liverpool to Preston line.

Above Mawdsley's shop facing the clock tower were boards announcing that they too stocked the famous gingerbread.

Swift's and the Corn Exchange on the corners of Moor Street and Market Row (see also p. 11). The rooms above the Exchange were often used for meetings and social gatherings.

Swift's shop later, in the 1920s, when the entrance had been moved to the centre of the shop and Swift's café had become a favourite rendezvous for morning coffee. The assistant in the centre of the picture is Ellen Hurst.

In the 1950s Swift's café became Swift's furniture stores, but retained the beautiful upper floors of the earlier shop.

Cammack's bottles. Cammack's mineral waters were another famous product of the town. The firm used a picture of Ormskirk Church as their trade mark and even the glass bottles with a marble in their 'throat' had the picture moulded in the glass. Cammack's factory later became the site of Hesford's iron foundry.

These lorries were used by Ellis Ward's Bath Springs Brewery. The natural spring water of the district gave the local ale its special taste, and, according to a seventeenth-century writer, the Ormskirk girls their beautiful complexions. This bill (below), issued in 1866, shows how long the brewery had been operating.

BATH SPRING BREWERY,

Fo. 41

Ormskirk, Dec. 6 1866

4th of

Mrs. Margaret Rimmer

Maghull

Dr.

TO THE TRUSTEES OF THE LATE

1865

PHILIP FORSHAW.

Aug: 12	To balance of a/c £	151.	11.	2½

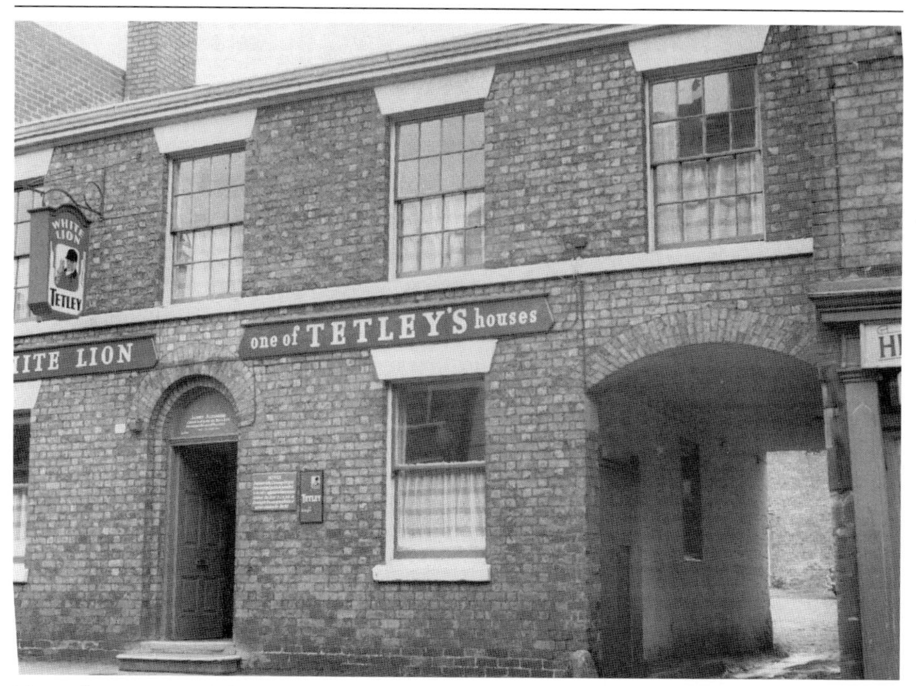

The White Lion in Church Street. The archway giving access to the inn yard was used by coaches in the nineteenth century.

The Greyhound, Aughton Street. The cottages alongside the inn have been demolished to make way for flats.

TELEPHONE 146. **HOTEL ESTABLISHED 200 YEARS.**

Headquarters Cyclists Touring Club.

Queen's Head Hotel, . . .

JOHN BANKS,
Proprietor.

Ormskirk.

EVERY ACCOMMODATION FOR FARMERS & VISITORS.

Parties Catered for. Bowling Green. Terms on application.

ORDINARY EVERY THURSDAY AT ONE O'CLOCK.

Wines and Spirits of the Finest Quality. Burton and other Ales on Draught.

... ... SPACIOUS YARD AND STABLING. ... ...

*** **This Hotel is one of the oldest in this part of Lancashire, having been in existence some 200 years, as the following extract from a book on "Some Old Country Sports in West Lancashire" (written by Nicholas Blundell, Esq., a relative of the Scarisbrick family) shows:—**

"1711, April 3. Coz. Scarisbrick and I and our wives went to a race on Aughton Moss, where a grey mare from Bretherton ran against a bay mare from towards Clitherow, &c. When the race was passed Mr. Scarisbrick and I went to Lancet's, the sign of the QUEEN'S HEAD IN ORMSKIRK, where we drank wine with Sir Thomas Stanley, Mr. Stanley his son, Captain Standish, Parson Hindley of Aughton, Mr. Ashurst, of Ashurst, &c."

This card advertises the Queen's Head and dates from the early 1920s. The 'ordinary' was a good meal favoured by visitors to the market since the early eighteenth century. Bowling, too, was a very popular game in that period.

The office of Idle and Stretch was located next to Gilbey's store.

PARTICULARS AND PLAN

OF

VALUABLE PROPERTY,

AT

AUGHTON, NEAR ORMSKIRK,

TO BE SOLD BY AUCTION,

BY MESSRS.

IDLE & STRETCH,

On THURSDAY, the 9th SEPTEMBER, 1880,

At 5 for 5.30 precisely in the Afternoon, at the

"WHEAT SHEAF HOTEL," ORMSKIRK,

Subject to Conditions of Sale to be seen at the Office of the Vendors' Solicitors seven days before the Sale

The auctioneers used the Wheat Sheaf for sales because their own premises were too small – and also because liquid refreshment was readily available. Forthcoming sales of property were advertised on boards outside their office. Later, this firm became Peter Freeman's.

The Wheat Sheaf was built in the eighteenth century. The elegant central staircase led to reception rooms decorated with intricate plasterwork. It was the venue for adjourned sessions of the court leet – until the court's dissolution in 1876, for meetings between lawyers and their clients, for important sales of property and for every kind of local celebration.

Billy Biggs outside his shop in Derby Street West, driving the first car to be sold in Ormskirk. It was bought by the Marquis de Casteja of Scarisbrick Hall. In the doorway are his wife, daughter and Jack Sumner, who later took over the garage and moved to Back Church Street.

Evidently the firm was not daunted by the prospect of supplying any form of motorized transport – even aeroplanes!

TO WIND UP AN ESTATE.

THURSDAY NEXT, MARCH 18, 1886,
AT 5·30 P.M.

WHEAT SHEAF INN, ORMSKIRK

Sale of Shares in the Ormskirk and Southport Building Society and in the Ormskirk Steam Corn Mills Company, Limited.

PETER FREEMAN

Is favoured with instructions to offer for SALE by AUCTION, at the time and place above-named (if not previously disposed of privately).

FIFTY £10

SHARES

IN THE ORMSKIRK & SOUTHPORT BUILDING SOCIETY,

SEVENTY £10 SHARES

(£5 PAID)

IN THE ORMSKIRK STEAM CORN MILLS COMPANY, LIMITED,
and which will be divided in lots to suit purchasers.

FURTHER PARTICULARS FROM THE AUCTIONEER, RAILWAY-ROAD, ORMSK[illegible]

Printed by T. HUTTON, at "The Advertiser" Steam-Printing Works, Church-st.

Here is a notice for a sale of shares, again at the Wheat Sheaf. The steam corn mill, the successor of a horse mill dating from the seventeenth century, was situated behind the shops in Church Street near Ball's iron foundry. In 1918 it caught fire and many schoolchildren were punished severely for playing truant from school to watch the blaze.

The old stone house, now Cornerstone's café, behind Burscough Street. Before it was converted, it was the workshop of Harry Cobham, the basketmaker. He used to collect willow saplings from alongside local brooks, soak them, strip off the bark and weave them into all kinds of hampers and baskets. This ancient building – shown on a 1609 map of Ormskirk – has been used for many purposes in its time. A piscina, in which altar vessels were washed, was found in one of the walls, so it is possible that it was once a chapel.

This carte-de-visite was produced by Wragg, the local photographer. Examples of his art were to be seen in this window of his shop at the top of Burscough Street.

A portrait of Mrs Banks, dressmaker, of Moor Street. Later, probably in the 1890s, Mrs Banks and her daughter moved to rooms over Garside's grocers, in Aughton Street. Their seamstresses made wedding dresses to order and, on the great day, were allowed time off work to watch the bride arrive in 'their' dress. When Alice Ashcroft worked there during the First World War, she was sent to Burscough camp to measure the officers' wives for their gowns for the Volunteers' Balls, held at the Drill Hall. The ladies often had their gowns remodelled for the next ball.

Burrows' drapery shop in Aughton Street. This shop, used by most of the dressmakers of the town in the early 1900s, later became Evans' and stood between Muggy Lea's pot shop and Williams' tailors. Evidently hand-knitted stockings were one of Burrows' specialities.

Aughton Street. A billboard advertising Williams' outfitters can be seen on the wall in the centre of the picture.

A page from a leaflet showing the garments sold by Williams at the turn of the century.

Williams' shop was between Burrows' and the post office. The family now has a men's outfitter's shop in Burscough Street.

No. 25 Aughton Street, the premises of Harry Burrows and his wife who were upholsterers. Ted Burrows, a plumber's merchant, used the back of the shop, which later became Cave's the confectioners, and still later, Draper's, also confectioners and caterers.

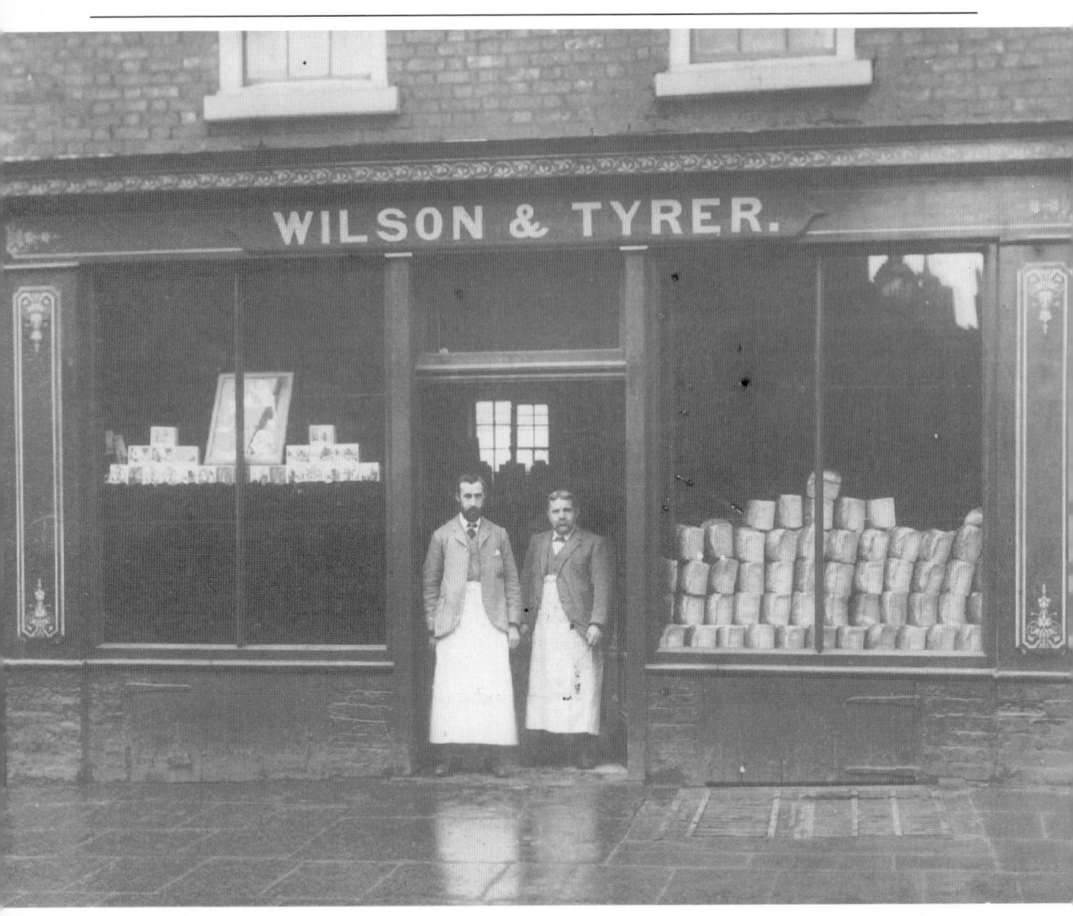

Wilson and Tyrer's shop was in Church Street. They were provender merchants who sold a wide range of animal food – anything from poultry corn to dog biscuits. The wooden shutters under the windows gave access to storerooms in the cellars.

In 1958 the firm moved to the shop next door. It had formerly been Tom Foster's, the pork butchers. Then John Naylor took over the shop and sold groceries, but retained the same name. The archway used to lead into one of Ormskirk's many courtyard developments.

John and Lottie Naylor pose inside the shop with their assistant.

Mansergh's hardware shop, which was one of those shops where local people were confident that they would find articles not available anywhere else. Mansergh's carried such a large stock that they had converted nearly every room of the premises into storerooms, and the smell of paraffin pervaded the whole place. Even today, years after they have left, a faint whiff of paraffin haunts the cellars.

Mr Jack Scott, the butcher, poses with his car outside the Town Green Inn in Aughton, late 1920s.

The slaughter yard was behind Scott's butchers in Church Street. Most butchers had their own slaughter yards in the early years of the twentieth century, but gradually slaughtering became more centralized and Mr Scott provided facilities for other butchers. Albert Huyton, grandfather of Howard Huyton, butcher of Town Green, holds the poleaxe ready to stun the short-horned bullock.

The cooper's workshop in Derby Street. Woosey's sold paraffin and firewood as well as barrels. Local people still remember the winter's day when Woosey's horse slipped and fell in the snow, and the barrels from the cart rolled all over the street.

At the other end of the terrace lived the Thompson family of furniture removers, who had a large yard at the rear. Here Harry, one of the seven Thompson brothers, is driving the van out of the yard.

John Thompson, founder of the firm, standing outside his home in Derby Street, 1920s. This house is occupied now by Harry, one of his grandsons.

Thompson's horse-drawn removal pantechnicon was used in the late nineteenth century and stored in the yard until recently.

Thompson's yard in the early 1900s. The horses had been decorated and were on their way to a parade following Tommy Sumner, who was leading the first horse. John Thompson is in the centre wearing an apron. Dennis Jackson, a carpenter, is standing

on his own in one of the upper doors, and among the boys at the other door is Richard Chadwick Thompson. Later these stables were bricked up to make furniture storerooms.

Garside's in Aughton Street next door to the Talbot Hotel. In this high class grocers, tea was stored in chests, butter was weighed from barrels and the smell of coffee filled the air. When a customer paid, the money was put into an overhead box which was sent along wires to the office. There the change was placed in the box and returned to the counter, much to the fascination of the younger customers.

Draper's stationers and steam-printers in Burscough Street, early 1900s. A billhead dating from 1897 lists Bibles, prayer-books, church services and hymn-books among their stock.

A market salesman in action, June 1949. Since that date most of the open stalls have been replaced by stalls with overhead awnings for protection against the weather.

The old bus station when Ribble operated the services in Ormskirk.

A scene in the market, 1949. This was before the King's Arms and several of the old shops had been demolished. In the immediate post-war years there were fewer stalls because food and other goods were still in short supply. In the foreground are Mr J. Taylor, then clerk of the council, Mrs Tootal and her granddaughter Sheila Longley.

Balmforth's garage stood next to the telephone exchange in Aughton Street before the firm moved to a bigger site on the other side of the road.

Section Four

SPECIAL OCCASIONS

A parade outside the Talbot in Aughton Street.

Tommy Sumner leading a decorated horse to join one of the many Ormskirk parades.

A parade of decorated horses and carts wending their way to join the carnival procession. The second horse belonged to Thompson's removal contractors.

A horse-drawn float at a carnival. The notice claims that it was sponsored by the *Ormskirk Advertiser* in aid of the youngsters' playground.

Another, more modern, float sponsored by Ormskirk Gas Company. At the wheel was Tommy Sumner who previously drove a horse and cart for the gasworks.

The next three pictures were taken at a very important parade during the 1930s. One of the banners reads 'Long May He Reign', and so it was probably the procession organized to celebrate the coronation of George VI.

The procession in Moor Street.

The procession in Aughton Street.

A Scout dance at the Institute, 1934. During the 1930s the Scouts organized a series of most successful dances, often engaging well-known bands to play and so attracting a large following.

A social organized by the Methodists in the upstairs room at Emmanuel Church, 1937. The minister in the centre is Revd W.G. Freeman, whose wife can be seen to the left of the garland on the back row.

After a Guide parade at the Parish Church, 1930s. Left to right: Ethelwynne Roberts, District Commissioner, Mary Leadbetter (later Allen), District Commissioner, Mrs Rushton, Divisional Commissioner for Wigan, Richard Edgerley, Chairman of the Council, Mrs Robertson Dodd, Divisional Commissioner for Ormskirk, and Lady Scarisbrick.

Lady Scarisbrick at the war memorial with a veteran.

Lady Scarisbrick reopening the Institute after its refurbishment, 1930s. The group includes Canon Redwood, John Close and his wife, and Archie Clucas.

Members of the British Legion selling poppies in the foyer of the Regal cinema – now Tesco. On the left is Mr A.P. Lea, secretary of the Legion, and on the right Mr Parkes of the Regal. No wonder so many people flocked to the cinemas when the price of seats was so low – 1*s* and 1*s* 6*d* for seats in the balcony.

A Remembrance Day parade, early 1930s. Alf Lea, who lost his hand during the First World War, can be seen holding the banner at the right-hand side of the drill hall steps. The group includes John Curtis, Major Lyon, Gill Norris, Bill Rigby, Les Prescott, George Sharrock and Bob Grayson.

Lord Derby unveiling the memorial to those lost in the Second World War. The vicar, Canon Redwood, is standing on the podium.

The Chairman of the Council's dinner, 1948. This was a double celebration, because Chairman Alf Lea's son, Norman, had recently returned from the forces after serving with the Life Guards and the Household Cavalry. Among the group are Mr and Mrs Les Haydock, Mrs Lee and Mr and Mrs Desmond Herne.

This group is at one of the comic carnivals held to raise money for various charities before the Second World War. Among them are Braithe Carter, Tommy Coleman, Billy Coleman, Mickey Winrow, Walter Foster, Bert Spencer, John Gibbons, John McDougall, Leo Wills and Harry Ormesher – in the centre wearing a bow tie.

Distributing food parcels sent from Canada to Ormskirk old age pensioners, 1949. To the right of the Chairman of the Council, Alf Lea, can be seen Mrs Knight, Welfare Officer, James Bell and Canon Redwood, and to the left Josiah Taylor, Clerk to the Council.

The saluting base at the Festival of Youth, 1950. The Chairman of the Council, Alf Lea, is watching the parade with his wife. Also in the group from left to right are Jim Webster, Albert Newall, Selby Worthington, Ada Lockwood Bunce, Jim Freeman, Barbara Parker and John Westhead.

Liverpool Scottish Pipers parading at the Festival of Youth, 1950.

A later chairman's dinner when Alf Lea was chairman for a second time in the 1960s. The group includes Mrs Ballance, Mrs Hughes, Howard Ballance, Glyn Hughes, chemist, A.P. Lee, Mrs Scott, Mr J. Scott, Mrs Lee, Mr Lee, Glyn Hughes, Mrs Hughes, Mrs Bird.

Choirmen from the Parish Church when Canon Grayson paid a visit there, *c.* 1954. Left to right: -?-, Mr Gerald Hogg, Mr Alan Beatty, Revd Canon Bob Grayson, Mr Wesley McCabe, Mr W. Kinsey, Mr Beatty, Mr Roby Hollinsworth.

William Burrows, who was Chairman of the Urban District Council, 1939–40.

After the wedding of John Culshaw, pharmacist, and Lilian Jackson, outside Fir Tree Cottage on Dyer's Lane, opposite the bottom of Ryburn Road, 1899. Nowadays the traffic rushes past, but then the older relatives could sit in chairs on the pavement while the photographer arranged the group to display those gorgeous clothes.

Section Five

YOUNG PEOPLE

A young cyclist in Ormskirk, 1920s.

An early Ormskirk schoolmaster. In 1861 Thomas S. Harper, his wife Ellen and their son, Thomas, taught the eighteen boys ranging in age from seven to sixteen who boarded at the Mansion House Academy on St Helens Road.

A class from Aughton Street Boys' School, 1910. The teacher in the photograph is Leonard Winder, headmaster of the school for thirty-four years, who died in 1921. He is commemorated by a plaque in the south aisle of the Parish Church.

Another class from Aughton Street Boys' School, late 1920s. To the right of the group is Mr Hunter, the headmaster at that time, who is remembered for being extremely strict and often using the cane. The other teacher is Eric Soar, who served as a fighter pilot in the Second World War. Among the boys are Benny Howe, ? Ollerton, ? Shorlicker and Bill Bibby.

Yet another class from Aughton Street Boys' School. Here the master is Mr Ball, who took the senior classes and specialized in history and English. He left Aughton Street to become headmaster at Bickerstaffe School and then moved to Melling.

The Girls' and Infants' National School in Derby Street. The front playground walls have since been removed and the building converted into Stoker's furniture shop.

Derby Street School at the end of the nineteenth century. Amy Burrows is one of the girls on the back row. The tight bodice, leg o'mutton sleeves and the long skirt of the teacher must have hampered her if she tried to do any active lessons with the children.

At Derby Street School, 1930s. Back row, left to right: -?-, Frank Johnson, William Blackledge, -?-, -?-, Ken Core, -?-, Harry Butterworth, -?-, -?-. Third row: Ronnie Scragg, -?-, -?-, Muriel Bennett, Marion Preece, -?-, -?-, Eileen Martland, -?-, -?-. Second row: Dennis Foster, -?-, Cliffe Ashton, Irene Berkley, Fred Taylor, Florence Parker, Roy Chadwick, Thelma Hale, Les Foster. Front row: -?-, Pierre Seddon, Ian Seddon, -?-, John Parker, Ronnie Dermott, -?-, -?-.

Derby Street School, 1928. Back row, left to right: Hazel Phipps, -?-, -?-, John Dickinson, -?-, Frank Booth. Middle row: -?-, Nora Hotchkiss, -?-, -?-, Jack Pearce, Gladys Foster, -?-. Front row: -?-, -?-, -?-, -?-, -?-, Joe Banks, Geoffrey Bliss.

Derby Street School, 1929. Back row, left to right: Gwen Rice, Edith Taylor, Ruth Clay, Connie Bimpson, Lily Leverton, Ethel Lea, Ethel Hudson, Ellen Seddon. Middle row: Dorothy Moss, Betty Alty, Florrie Wade, Doris Orritt, Phyllis Moorcroft, Joan Molyneux. Front row: Elsie Whittle, Ethel Finch, Edie Rimmer, Marion Orritt, Ethel Small, Winnie Huyton, Alice Sanderson.

A group of grammar school pupils after a dramatic production, 1935. Among the cast is Eric Bromley, in the centre wearing a top hat.

A group from the production of *Twelfth Night* by pupils from Hants Lane School, 1920s. The actors are, from left to right: Raymond Ashcroft, Marie Wills, Alfred Kenny, May Gore, Joe Smith, Raymond Winrow, Charlie Rylance.

A class in Wigan Road School, 1935. Back row, left to right: Edna Morgan, Betty Brookfield, Gertie Hardman, Dorothy Seddon, May Rasburn, Phyllis Foster, Hazel Phipps, Edna Ashcroft, Teresa Royle, Olwyn Hancock, Freda Tromp. Third row: Alice Pendlebury, Stella Baker, Hazel Rice, Eunice Appleton, Alice Johnson, Myrtle Twist, Evelyn Griffiths, Brenda Green, Vera Banks. Second row: Audrey Pilkington, Kathleen Jeeves, Evelyn Berkley, Doris Foster, Brenda Crompton, Eleanor Jaeger, Jean Rawsthorn, Margaret Tweddle, Vera Godfry, Joan Baldwin. Front row: Joan Dawson, Doris Banks, Edith Jackson, Gladys Nelson, Betty Harvey, Eva Tootal, Eileen Willetts, Edith Johnson, Joan Maudsley, Lilian Davis.

St Anne's morris dancers, 1920s. Back row, left to right: Delia Ashby, Kathleen O'Neill, Kathleen Doran, Marie Makin, Mary Gore, Nancy Judge, Marie Whalley, Josie Howard, Norah Stewart, Mary Walmesley, Rosie Gaffney, Josie Woods, Ivy Morley, Cissie Mawdsley, Mary Staniforth. Front row: Alicia Finnegan, Bertha Ashley, Joan Westhead, Norah Kerrigan, Winnie Ball, Nancy Ball, Marie Wills, Ronnie Davies, Nancy McKenna.

Morris dancing by the Belles of Aughton from Christ Church School, 1929. The setting was Moss Bank, the home of the Hutton family in Long Lane, Aughton. The occasion was a summer gala organized by Harold Hutton on behalf of Ormskirk Scouts.

After the opening of the Scout headquarters in Wigan Road. The uniforms and backpacks of the Scouts contrast sharply with today's uniforms.

A group of Scouts and their leaders outside their headquarters, 1926. Seated: Eric Soar, Norman Goodacre, Fred Muir, Vera Muir, Mr Mahood, the Revd Mr Lansley, Mr Torr, Mr Hutton, Mrs Mahood, May Sumner, Eric Ponsonby, Jack Seddon, John Prescott, George Allen.

1st Ormskirk Scouts camping in Anglesey, 1946. Left to right: -?-, Ken Sumner, -?-, ? Taylor, ? Bracegirdle, Len Kenny, John Blundell (Scoutmaster), ? Kenny, Richard Moss (Assistant Scoutmaster), Roy Sawyer, Harold Hutton, Raymond Bladen, -?-, Roy Huyton, -?-, Fred Taylor.

The 5th Ormskirk Scouts and Cubs camping on the Ellerbrook Camp site, early 1940s. The caravan belonged to the 1st Ormskirk Scouts and was kept at the Lathom camp site. Seated in the centre are Marjorie Woods, Winnie Bimpson and Mary Robinson (Cub mistresses), Bob Roscoe, Bob Hesketh, Noel Horner, Bert Skaife and Tom Mahoney. Barry Stockton is holding the Cub flag. Also included in the group are Peter Ingram, Ronnie Scragg, Michael Evans, Frank Shepherd, Peter and Gerald Howe, Charlie Thompson, Trevor Saunders and Peter Birkhill.

Ormskirk Rover Scouts, 1930s. Back row, left to right: ? Cardus, Mr Hutton, Jack Crompton, John Moran, Eric Moss. Middle row: Charles Anderton, Jack Sumner, Joe Webster, Harold Sumner. Front row: Eric Soar, Harry Kaye, ? Rurton, Jack Griffiths.

All packed up and ready to return from camp at Arrowe Park, 1928.

The chorus line of Rover Scouts, 1930s. On the ground: ? Seddon. Left to right: Norman Smith, Alan McRae, Eric Moss, Harold Sumner, Joe Webster, John Moran, Bernard Fitzpatrick, Percy Hutton.

Rover Scout Norman Smith making use of the rural amenities near the camp.

A group of Scouts in front of the Ormskirk cottage hospital ambulance, which served as a first aid post on field days. Left to right: John Prescott, Jack Crompton, Joe Webster, Bernard Fitzpatrick, George Allen, Charles Anderton.

Ormskirk Scouts marching behind the town band and passing the King's Arms. Mr Torr, District Commissioner, and Mr Harold Hutton are leading the contingent.

Outside the Scout headquarters when Lord Rowallan visited Ormskirk. Harold Hutton accompanied him as he reviewed Scouts from all over the area. Ken Sumner is one of the guards of honour in the photograph.

May Sumner with her Cubs, late 1920s.

A young Cub being convinced that even Cub leaders wash their faces – Lathom Park camp, 1935.

Ormskirk Cubs arriving at Whitewell in one of Gore's coaches for their summer camp, 1931.

1st Ormskirk Cubs marching through Ormskirk market, late 1920s. Among the crowd watching the parade from the back of the butchers' stalls is Mrs Ablett from the shoe shop.

The 1st Ormskirk Guides with their captain Mary Allen marching down Southport Road, 1930s. Possibly it was an Armistice Day procession following a route from the cenotaph to the Parish Church.

A 21st birthday celebration for the 1st Ormskirk Guides, 1936. Left to right: Barbara Bloomfield, Minnie Crossley, Ada Leadbetter, Dorothy Ball, Nora Townsend, Mary Allen (Captain).

Emmanuel Methodist Church Primary department with Miss Harriet Evans and Mrs Nora Booth (née Townsend), 1936. The little boy in braces on the front row is Fred Taylor.

,The choir outside the Parish Church, 8 May 1938. Among the adults are, left to right on the back row: -?-, Mr Roby Hollinsworth, Mr Dodd, -?-. Seated: -?-, Mr Jim Leatherbarrow, -?-, Mr Eveson, Mr Freeman (churchwarden), Canon F.A. Redwood (vicar), Mr Cowan (curate), Mr Edward Bamber (organist and choirmaster), Mr Sam Orritt (sexton), Mr F. Bates, -?-.

Mrs Blundell crowning Dorothy Hargraves the Rose Queen at the Scouts' carnival, May 1939.

The Rose Queen procession on the cow field in Derby Street opposite Emmanuel Church. Among the crowd are Fred Anyon and his wife Madge (née Taylor). In the background are tanks of water for the steam trains in the station.

Section Six

FROM THE DISTRICTS

Enjoying camp at Lathom.

The Stanley Gate at Bickerstaffe. The town band used to practise in the cottage behind the inn and bandsmen remember that the tempo quickened as the night progressed. I wonder whether that was the result of liquid refreshment.

High Farm, Bickerstaffe, 1890s. Deborah, wife of Richard Rimmer, the farmer, is standing at the front while Kate, her only daughter, can be seen at the side with their servant, Elizabeth Peet of Skelmersdale. Later the walls of the house were rendered and whitened.

Bath Lodge. This was built in the early eighteenth century by the Honourable Charles Stanley, the brother of the Earl of Derby, to house a cold plunge bath. Walks were laid out and it was hoped that a spa might develop around it, but it never became popular.

The Martland family outside Bath Farm. On the left is Fred, who died of 'flu as a young man, and with him are his sisters Alice and Jane.

The windmill on Holborn Hill, Aughton. The chimney was built when a steam engine was installed to speed up the milling process.

Haymaking on Clieves Hill, Aughton. John Huyton is driving the horses and Joseph Robinson is standing beside him.

Christ Church May Queen, early 1930s. The queen was Margaret Balmer and one of her maids of honour was Mary Robinson. Peggy Silcock from Aughton Springs crowned the queen on Trench field at the corner of Prescot Road and Long Lane.

William Bevan's butcher's shop in Town Green, Aughton. The iron railings were taken for the war effort during the Second World War. At this time William Bevan employed Albert Huyton, whose son Sidney later joined the staff, finally taking over the business in 1952.

The shops near the railway bridge at Town Green, Aughton. They included a grocery, a pharmacy, a haberdasher, a greengrocer and a butcher. Every need could be supplied from that one terrace.

Aughton Cricket Club, 1910. Back row, left to right: H. Grantham, A. Cropper, W. Bevan, Joseph Draper, W. Grantham, T. Taylor, J. Harrocks. Middle row: J.E. Allen sen., E. Nottingham, D. Draper, J.E. Allen, jun., Robert Draper (Captain), John Sephton, E. Draper (Hon. Secretary), John Draper, J. Lake. Front row: T. Bowling, E. Ashcroft.

Downholland Hall with Mrs Bond in her sun-bonnet. The interior of this hall, which dates from Tudor times, has recently been gutted and modernized.

Haskayne village street. Hollies Farm and barn can be seen at the end of the lane. One of these cottages was used as a mission in the 1920s.

The Blue Bell at Barton, a popular stop for both cart-horses and their drivers. The building has had very few alterations since the 1920s.

A committee from West Lancashire Council inspecting the roads. They had stopped outside the church in Halsall for the picture. Certainly the solid tyres of the charabanc would test the smoothness of the road surfaces.

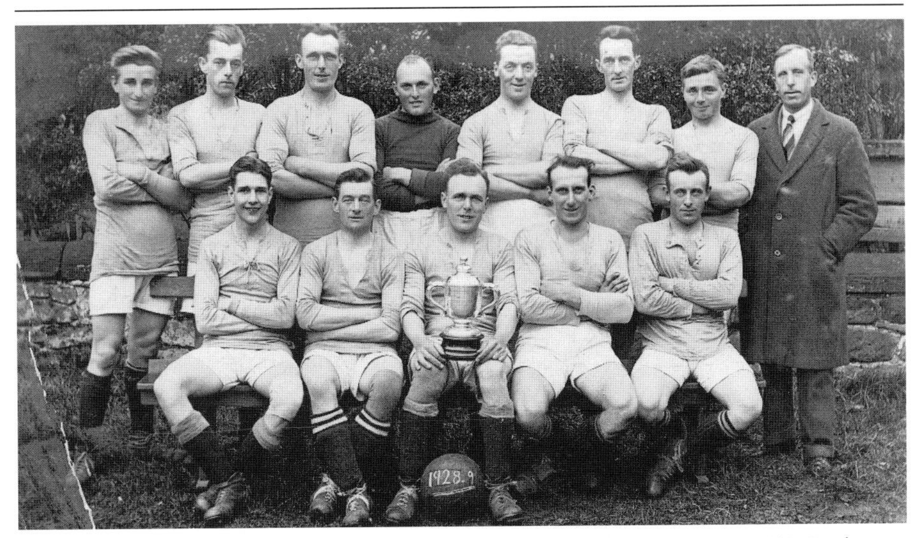

Halsall Amateur Football Club, winners of the Colonel White Cup in 1928/9. Back row, left to right: J. Massam, J. Huyton, J. Threlfall, M. Neale, G. Porter, W. Oswald (captain), J. Sefton, J. Fraser (trainer). Front row: G. McCoy, W. Martindale, T. Threlfall, J. Abram, T. Hurst.

The Saracen's Head at Halsall, 1930s. The landlord was Mr Sharrock who ran a bus to Liverpool market. He drove around the farms between 3 a.m. and 4 a.m. collecting anyone who wanted to go to the market to buy or to sell, and took them into the city.

A rally outside the Swan Hotel at Aughton taken by Wragg, the Ormskirk photographer, at the end of the nineteenth century. The cars were on a trial run from Liverpool and called at the Swan on the way.

1

Men with a steamroller repairing the road near Shaw Brook Bridge, 1920s.

Lathom House was built in the early eighteenth century as the home of the Earls of Derby. During the First World War, the house was used as a remount depot and was so badly damaged that it was decided not to repair it. Now only the ruined stable block remains.

BRITAIN IN OLD PHOTOGRAPHS

To order any of these titles please telephone Littlehampton Book Services on 01903 721596

ALDERNEY

Alderney: A Second Selection, *B Bonnard*

BEDFORDSHIRE

Bedfordshire at Work, *N Lutt*

BERKSHIRE

Maidenhead, *M Hayles & D Hedges*
Around Maidenhead, *M Hayles & B Hedges*
Reading, *P Southerton*
Reading: A Second Selection, *P Southerton*
Sandhurst and Crowthorne, *K Dancy*
Around Slough, *J Hunter & K Hunter*
Around Thatcham, *P Allen*
Around Windsor, *B Hedges*

BUCKINGHAMSHIRE

Buckingham and District, *R Cook*
High Wycombe, *R Goodearl*
Around Stony Stratford, *A Lambert*

CHESHIRE

Cheshire Railways, *M Hitches*
Chester, *S Nichols*

CLWYD

Clwyd Railways, *M Hitches*

CLYDESDALE

Clydesdale, *Lesmahagow Parish Historical Association*

CORNWALL

Cornish Coast, *T Bowden*
Falmouth, *P Gilson*
Lower Fal, *P Gilson*
Around Padstow, *M McCarthy*
Around Penzance, *J Holmes*
Penzance and Newlyn, *J Holmes*
Around Truro, *A Lyne*
Upper Fal, *P Gilson*

CUMBERLAND

Cockermouth and District, *J Bernard Bradbury*
Keswick and the Central Lakes, *J Marsh*
Around Penrith, *F Boyd*
Around Whitehaven, *H Fancy*

DERBYSHIRE

Derby, *D Buxton*
Around Matlock, *D Barton*

DEVON

Colyton and Seaton, *T Gosling*
Dawlish and Teignmouth, *G Gosling*
Devon Aerodromes, *K Saunders*
Exeter, *P Thomas*
Exmouth and Budleigh Salterton, *T Gosling*
From Haldon to Mid-Dartmoor, *T Hall*
Honiton and the Otter Valley, *J Yallop*
Around Kingsbridge, *K Tanner*
Around Seaton and Sidmouth, *T Gosling*
Seaton, Axminster and Lyme Regis, *T Gosling*

DORSET

Around Blandford Forum, *B Cox*
Bournemouth, *M Colman*
Bridport and the Bride Valley, *J Burrell & S Humphries*
Dorchester, *T Gosling*
Around Gillingham, *P Crocker*

DURHAM

Darlington, *G Flynn*
Darlington: A Second Selection, *G Flynn*
Durham People, *M Richardson*
Houghton-le-Spring and Hetton-le-Hole, *K Richardson*
Houghton-le-Spring and Hetton-le-Hole: A Second Selection, *K Richardson*
Sunderland, *S Miller & B Bell*
Teesdale, *D Coggins*
Teesdale: A Second Selection, *P Raine*
Weardale, *J Crosby*
Weardale: A Second Selection, *J Crosby*

DYFED

Aberystwyth and North Ceredigion, *Dyfed Cultural Services Dept*
Haverfordwest, *Dyfed Cultural Services Dept*
Upper Tywi Valley, *Dyfed Cultural Services Dept*

ESSEX

Around Grays, *B Evans*

GLOUCESTERSHIRE

Along the Avon from Stratford to Tewkesbury, *J Jeremiah*
Cheltenham: A Second Selection, *R Whiting*
Cheltenham at War, *P Gill*
Cirencester, *J Welsford*
Around Cirencester, *E Cuss & P Griffiths*
Forest, The, *D Mullin*
Gloucester, *J Voyce*
Around Gloucester, *A Sutton*
Gloucester: From the Walwin Collection, *J Voyce*
North Cotswolds, *D Viner*
Severn Vale, *A Sutton*
Stonehouse to Painswick, *A Sutton*
Stroud and the Five Valleys, *S Gardiner & L Padin*
Stroud and the Five Valleys: A Second Selection, *S Gardiner & L Padin*
Stroud's Golden Valley, *S Gardiner & L Padin*
Stroudwater and Thames & Severn Canals, *E Cuss & S Gardiner*
Stroudwater and Thames & Severn Canals: A Second Selection, *E Cuss & S Gardiner*
Tewkesbury and the Vale of Gloucester, *C Hilton*
Thornbury to Berkeley, *J Hudson*
Uley, Dursley and Cam, *A Sutton*
Wotton-under-Edge to Chipping Sodbury, *A Sutton*

GWYNEDD

Anglesey, *M Hitches*
Gwynedd Railways, *M Hitches*
Around Llandudno, *M Hitches*
Vale of Conwy, *M Hitches*

HAMPSHIRE

Gosport, *J Sadden*
Portsmouth, *P Rogers & D Francis*

HEREFORDSHIRE

Herefordshire, *A Sandford*

HERTFORDSHIRE

Barnet, *I Norrie*
Hitchin, *A Fleck*
St Albans, *S Mullins*
Stevenage, *M Appleton*

ISLE OF MAN

The Tourist Trophy, *B Snelling*

ISLE OF WIGHT

Newport, *D Parr*
Around Ryde, *D Parr*

JERSEY

Jersey: A Third Selection, *R Lemprière*

KENT

Bexley, *M Scott*
Broadstairs and St Peter's, *J Whyman*
Bromley, Keston and Hayes, *M Scott*
Canterbury: A Second Selection, *D Butler*
Chatham and Gillingham, *P MacDougall*
Chatham Dockyard, *P MacDougall*
Deal, *J Broady*
Early Broadstairs and St Peter's, *B Wootton*
East Kent at War, *D Collyer*
Eltham, *J Kennett*
Folkestone: A Second Selection, *A Taylor & E Rooney*
Goudhurst to Tenterden, *A Guilmant*
Gravesend, *R Hiscock*
Around Gravesham, *R Hiscock & D Grierson*
Herne Bay, *J Hawkins*
Lympne Airport, *D Collyer*
Maidstone, *I Hales*
Margate, *R Clements*
RAF Hawkinge, *R Humphreys*
RAF Manston, *RAF Manston History Club*
RAF Manston: A Second Selection, *RAF Manston History Club*
Ramsgate and Thanet Life, *D Perkins*
Romney Marsh, *E Carpenter*
Sandwich, *C Wanostrocht*
Around Tonbridge, *C Bell*
Tunbridge Wells, *M Rowlands & I Beavis*
Tunbridge Wells: A Second Selection, *M Rowlands & I Beavis*
Around Whitstable, *C Court*
Wingham, Adisham and Littlebourne, *M Crane*

LANCASHIRE

Around Barrow-in-Furness, *J Garbutt & J Marsh*
Blackpool, *C Rothwell*
Bury, *J Hudson*
Chorley and District, *J Smith*
Fleetwood, *C Rothwell*
Heywood, *J Hudson*
Around Kirkham, *C Rothwell*
Lancashire North of the Sands, *J Garbutt & J Marsh*
Around Lancaster, *S Ashworth*
Lytham St Anne's, *C Rothwell*
North Fylde, *C Rothwell*
Radcliffe, *J Hudson*
Rossendale, *B Moore & N Dunnachie*

LEICESTERSHIRE

Around Ashby-de-la-Zouch, *K Hillier*
Charnwood Forest, *I Keil, W Humphrey & D Wix*
Leicester, *D Burton*
Leicester: A Second Selection, *D Burton*
Melton Mowbray, *T Hickman*
Around Melton Mowbray, *T Hickman*
River Soar, *D Wix, P Shacklock & I Keil*
Rutland, *T Clough*
Vale of Belvoir, *T Hickman*
Around the Welland Valley, *S Mastoris*

LINCOLNSHIRE

Grimsby, *J Tierney*
Around Grimsby, *J Tierney*
Grimsby Docks, *J Tierney*
Lincoln, *D Cuppleditch*

Scunthorpe, *D Taylor*
Skegness, *W Kime*
Around Skegness, *W Kime*

LONDON

Balham and Tooting, *P Loobey*
Crystal Palace, Penge & Anerley, *M Scott*
Greenwich and Woolwich, *K Clark*
Hackney: A Second Selection, *D Mander*
Lewisham and Deptford, *J Coulter*
Lewisham and Deptford: A Second Selection, *J Coulter*
Streatham, *P Loobey*
Around Whetstone and North Finchley, *J Heathfield*
Woolwich, *B Evans*

MONMOUTHSHIRE

Chepstow and the River Wye, *A Rainsbury*
Monmouth and the River Wye, *Monmouth Museum*

NORFOLK

Great Yarmouth, *M Teun*
Norwich, *M Colman*
Wymondham and Attleborough, *P Yaxley*

NORTHAMPTONSHIRE

Around Stony Stratford, *A Lambert*

NOTTINGHAMSHIRE

Arnold and Bestwood, *M Spick*
Arnold and Bestwood: A Second Selection, *M Spick*
Changing Face of Nottingham, *G Oldfield*
Mansfield, *Old Mansfield Society*
Around Newark, *T Warner*
Nottingham: 1944–1974, *D Whitworth*
Sherwood Forest, *D Ottewell*
Victorian Nottingham, *M Payne*

OXFORDSHIRE

Around Abingdon, *P Horn*
Banburyshire, *M Barnett & S Gosling*
Burford, *A Jewell*
Around Didcot and the Hagbournes, *B Lingham*
Garsington, *M Gunther*
Around Henley-on-Thames, *S Ellis*
Oxford: The University, *J Rhodes*
Thame to Watlington, *N Hood*
Around Wallingford, *D Beasley*
Witney, *T Worley*
Around Witney, *C Mitchell*
Witney District, *T Worley*
Around Woodstock, *J Bond*

POWYS

Brecon, *Brecknock Museum*
Welshpool, *E Bredsdorff*

SHROPSHIRE

Shrewsbury, *D Trumper*
Whitchurch to Market Drayton, *M Morris*

SOMERSET

Bath, *J Hudson*
Bridgwater and the River Parrett, *R Fitzhugh*
Bristol, *D Moorcroft & N Campbell-Sharp*
Changing Face of Keynsham,
B Lowe & M Whitehead
Chard and Ilminster, *G Gosling & F Huddy*
Crewkerne and the Ham Stone Villages,
G Gosling & F Huddy
Around Keynsham and Saltford, *B Lowe & T Brown*
Midsomer Norton and Radstock, *C Howell*
Somerton, Ilchester and Langport, *G Gosling & F Huddy*
Taunton, *N Chipchase*
Around Taunton, *N Chipchase*
Wells, *C Howell*
Weston-Super-Mare, *S Poole*
Around Weston-Super-Mare, *S Poole*
West Somerset Villages, *K Houghton & L Thomas*

STAFFORDSHIRE

Aldridge, *J Farrow*
Bilston, *E Rees*
Black Country Transport: Aviation, *A Brew*
Around Burton upon Trent, *G Sowerby & R Farman*
Bushbury, *A Chatwin, M Mills & E Rees*
Around Cannock, *M Mills & S Belcher*
Around Leek, *R Poole*
Lichfield, *H Clayton & K Simmons*
Around Pattingham and Wombourne, *M Griffiths,*
P Leigh & M Mills
Around Rugeley, *T Randall & J Anslow*
Smethwick, *J Maddison*
Stafford, *J Anslow & T Randall*
Around Stafford, *J Anslow & T Randall*
Stoke-on-Trent, *I Lawley*
Around Tamworth, *R Sulima*
Around Tettenhall and Codsall, *M Mills*
Tipton, Wednesbury and Darlaston, *R Pearson*
Walsall, *D Gilbert & M Lewis*
Wednesbury, *I Bott*
West Bromwich, *R Pearson*

SUFFOLK

Ipswich: A Second Selection, *D Kindred*
Around Ipswich, *D Kindred*
Around Mildenhall, *C Dring*
Southwold to Aldeburgh, *H Phelps*
Around Woodbridge, *H Phelps*

SURREY

Cheam and Belmont, *P Berry*
Croydon, *S Bligh*
Dorking and District, *K Harding*
Around Dorking, *A Jackson*
Around Epsom, *P Berry*
Farnham: A Second Selection, *J Parratt*
Around Haslemere and Hindhead, *T Winter & G Collyer*
Richmond, *Richmond Local History Society*
Sutton, *P Berry*

SUSSEX

Arundel and the Arun Valley, *J Godfrey*
Bishopstone and Seaford, *P Pople & P Berry*
Brighton and Hove, *J Middleton*
Brighton and Hove: A Second Selection, *J Middleton*
Around Crawley, *M Goldsmith*
Hastings, *P Haines*
Hastings: A Second Selection, *P Haines*
Around Haywards Heath, *J Middleton*
Around Heathfield, *A Gillet & B Russell*
Around Heathfield: A Second Selection,
A Gillet & B Russell
High Weald, *B Harwood*
High Weald: A Second Selection, *B Harwood*
Horsham and District, *T Wales*
Lewes, *J Middleton*
RAF Tangmere, *A Saunders*
Around Rye, *A Dickinson*
Around Worthing, *S White*

WARWICKSHIRE

Along the Avon from Stratford to Tewkesbury, *J Jen*
Bedworth, *J Burton*
Coventry, *D McGrory*
Around Coventry, *D McGrory*
Nuneaton, *S Clews & S Vaughan*
Around Royal Leamington Spa, *J Cameron*
Around Royal Leamington Spa: A Second Selectio
J Cameron
Around Warwick, *R Booth*

WESTMORLAND

Eden Valley, *J Marsh*
Kendal, *M & P Duff*
South Westmorland Villages, *J Marsh*
Westmorland Lakes, *J Marsh*

WILTSHIRE

Around Amesbury, *P Daniels*
Chippenham and Lacock, *A Wilson & M Wilson*
Around Corsham and Box, *A Wilson & M Wilson*
Around Devizes, *D Buxton*
Around Highworth, *G Tanner*
Around Highworth and Faringdon, *G Tanner*
Around Malmesbury, *A Wilson*
Marlborough: A Second Selection, *P Colman*
Around Melksham,
Melksham and District Historical Association
Nadder Valley, *R. Sawyer*
Salisbury, *P Saunders*
Salisbury: A Second Selection, *P Daniels*
Salisbury: A Third Selection, *P Daniels*
Around Salisbury, *P Daniels*
Swindon: A Third Selection, *The Swindon Society*
Swindon: A Fourth Selection, *The Swindon Society*
Trowbridge, *M Marshman*
Around Wilton, *P Daniels*
Around Wootton Bassett, Cricklade and Purton, *T Sharp*

WORCESTERSHIRE

Evesham to Bredon, *F Archer*
Around Malvern, *K Smith*
Around Pershore, *M Dowty*
Redditch and the Needle District, *R Saunders*
Redditch: A Second Selection, *R Saunders*
Around Tenbury Wells, *D Green*
Worcester, *M Dowty*
Around Worcester, *R Jones*
Worcester in a Day, *M Dowty*
Worcestershire at Work, *R Jones*

YORKSHIRE

Huddersfield: A Second Selection, *H Wheeler*
Huddersfield: A Third Selection, *H Wheeler*
Leeds Road and Rail, *R Vickers*
Pontefract, *R van Riel*
Scarborough, *D Coggins*
Scarborough's War Years, *R Percy*
Skipton and the Dales, *Friends of the Craven Museum*
Around Skipton-in-Craven, *Friends of the Craven Museum*
Yorkshire Wolds, *I & M Sumner*

Halogen Oven Cookbook

The Halogen Oven Cookbook
Compiled by Paul Jones and Leah Meads
ISBN: 978-0-9551674-3-0

Bookworm of Retford 2009

www.thehalogenovencookbook.co.uk
info@thehalogenovencookbook.co.uk

Cover, logo and photo design: Leah Georgette Photography
Bookworm of Retford
1 Spa Lane
Retford
Nottinghamshire
DN22 6EA

Printed and bound by Burgess Design and Print, Retford

Bookworm of Retford

Contents

- Hints and Tips 3
- Cooking Vegetables 6
- Cooking Meat 8
- Vegetable Pasta Bake 10
- Quick and Easy Pasta 12
- Roasted Peppers 14
- Broccoli and Mixed Cheese Quiche 16
- Roast Chicken Dinner 18
- Mediterranean Chicken 20
- Chicken Escalopes 22
- Pork Steaks with Honey Glazed Apple Slices 24
- Marinated Pork Chops 26
- Beef Casserole 28
- Roast Beef with Roasted Vegetables 30
- Homemade Burgers 32
- Tartiflette 34
- Baked Cod 36
- Salmon with Ratatouille 38
- Something Tasty on Toast 40
- Welsh Rarebit 42
- Potato Dauphinoise 44
- Olive Bread 46
- Roast Potatoes 48
- Cheesy Biscuits 50
- Apple and Blackberry Bake 52
- Cupcakes 54
- Afternoon Tea Scones 56
- Mincemeat and Apple Slice 58
- Conversion Chart 60

Hints and Tips

Whilst we have thoroughly checked our cooking times for our recipes, always ensure food is piping hot before serving. You should also refer to your manufacturer's instructions for operational and maintenance instructions. However, we have a few hints and tips to help you make the most of your Halogen Oven.

★ Time Saving

The main feature of the Halogen Oven is that it reduces cooking times. Most of this time is saved in the preheating stage, as it takes next to no time for the heating element and the rest of the oven to reach the desired temperature. Most of the recipes here are easy to follow and involve mainly one-pot cooking. By the time you have prepared all your ingredients, your oven will be at the required temperature.

★ Using the Cooking Racks

As the heating element is at the top of the oven, the food on the higher cooking rack will cook more quickly than on the bottom cooking rack. The higher rack will cook food in a similar way to a grill; food placed on the lower rack will bake and roast. Vegetables that are to be roasted do not need a cooking rack and can be placed straight onto the base of your Halogen Oven.

★ Finishing Touches

There are many other benefits to using a Halogen Oven aside from the economical and time-saving factors. As the heat comes from above the food, it is great at adding nice crispy, golden finishes to things like pies with mashed potato or pastry toppings. Also, most of the recipes in this book are cooked in just one pot and involve baking, roasting or braising; this often eliminates the need for large amounts of fats like oils and butter, although small amounts of olive oil are used frequently to help prevent food from drying out.

★ Additional Cooking Space

Your Halogen Oven can also be used as an additional cooking space when your normal oven is already full. Why not use it to do the roast potatoes for a Sunday lunch, or broccoli and cauliflower gratin to accompany a casserole?

★ Care of the Heating Element

The heating element is delicate so requires special care. The lid should always be left to cool before cleaning. It shouldn't get too dirty during cooking, so a quick wipe will suffice, but don't rinse it, simply dry with a cloth. Also, when taking the top off the Halogen Oven in order to test the food, simply place it on a suitably sized heat-proof mat. Covering the mat in tinfoil gives added protection.

★ Experiment

The Halogen Oven works in much the same way as a conventional oven: anything that can be baked, roasted, grilled or braised in a conventional oven can be done in the Halogen Oven! Have the confidence to experiment with your cooking as the Halogen Oven is amazingly gentle and does not burn food easily. You can always see what is happening through the glass bowl; just keep testing the food until it is cooked.

★ Useful Accessories

To make using your Halogen Oven even easier, here are some common kitchen accessories that will be very useful:

- Tinfoil (to wrap and steam small portions of vegetables and to protect the top of meat from overcooking)
- Small roasting tin approx 26cm (10 –11 inches)
- Oven-proof casserole dish approx 26cm (10-11 inches)
- A round pizza tray, great for chips and potato wedges and pizzas!, approx 28cm (11 inches)
- Heat-proof mat, on which to stand the lid when it's hot
- Oven gloves: your Halogen Oven will get very hot!
- Tongs for turning food

★ Defrosting

Turn the dial to the 'defrost' or 'thaw' setting. For small items such as bread rolls and sliced bread, set the timer to 5 minutes but keep checking your food regularly. For meat portions and frozen meals set the timer to 10 minutes, adding further minutes as required. Food defrosted in a Halogen Oven may start to get warm and should therefore be cooked immediately after defrosting.

★ Timing guide

Each recipe shows a number of clocks indicating how long it will take to prepare and cook the dish.

30 minutes or less	🕓
1 hour or less	🕓🕓
Over 1 hour	🕓🕓🕓

These recipes have been tested in a 12 litre Halogen Oven. Please ensure you check your manufacturer's guide for preheating times for smaller ovens.

Use these hints and tips as a guide, but always refer to your manufacturer's instructions and ensure food is thoroughly heated before serving.

Don't forget that cooking times will depend on the size and cut of the pieces of meat, poultry, and fish and also by how fresh your ingredients are. You should cook to suit your personal tastes.

Cooking Vegetables

Vegetables are not often the main star of a dish, but if they are not cooked well can ruin an otherwise great meal. By giving yourself plenty of time to prepare them, you can ensure they always cook well and become a regular addition to your Halogen Oven.

Cook vegetables at 200°C on the low rack or on the base of the glass bowl.

★ Small Portions of Vegetables

Small portions of green vegetables can be cooked along with any meat in your cooker. Green vegetables such as peas, green beans or broccoli are best cooked wrapped in tin foil with a tbsp or two of water. This way, they will retain their moisture, colour and nutrients:

The following vegetables are ideally cooked wrapped in tinfoil:

peas	10-15	minutes
broccoli	20	minutes
cauliflower	20	minutes

★ Root Vegetables

Root vegetables such as carrots, swede, parsnips, leeks and celeriac, etc. can be roasted in the bottom of the glass bowl. Simply cut or slice them into bite-sized chunks; the smaller you cut them, the quicker they will cook. However, be careful not to cut them too small or they will lose their texture and shape. Roasting root vegetables like this will take up to an hour; parboiling for 8-10 minutes will reduce the roasting times by approximately 25-30 minutes.

★ Using Olive Oil on your Vegetables

Vegetables such as tomatoes, peppers, red onions and even garlic are at their best when roasted in a little olive oil. Cut them into similar sizes so they cook evenly; toss in a few whole garlic cloves. Leave the skins on the cloves and roast for 20 minutes. When ready, squeeze the garlic out of their skins and serve with meat or fish.

★ Broccoli and Cauliflower Gratin

Cook at 200°C.

Broccoli and cauliflower gratin is really simple. Cut the vegetables into florets and boil for 3 minutes in boiling, salted water. While they are boiling mix 6 tbsp of double cream with 2 egg yolks and set aside. Drain the vegetables and place in a suitably sized heatproof dish; then pour over the cream and egg mixture, season with salt, pepper and Parmesan cheese and bake for 15 minutes or until golden brown and the cheese is bubbling nicely.

★ Jacket Potatoes

Wash and then pierce the potatoes several times with a fork. Cook for 60 minutes at 200°C. After 45 minutes start checking the potatoes to see if they are cooked.

★ Experiment

Use the times given in this book to create your own meal ideas. Prepare all your ingredients, roast your chosen vegetables and then grill your meat on top. The juice from the meat will add a great flavour to the vegetables.

Cooking Meat

When roasting meat it is a good idea to wrap it in tinfoil or use a roasting tray with a foil lid. By doing this, the meat will cook evenly with no risk of burning, and all the delicious cooking juices will be collected in the foil or tin, rather than collect at the bottom of the glass bowl. Half-way through cooking and once there is a build up of the juices, turn the meat over. This allows all the juices to filter down through the meat, basting it as it goes! This is very important as it helps keep the meat succulent and moist without the need for constant basting.

Gammon Steaks

- 2 gammon steaks. Serves 2

Preheat the Halogen Oven to 200°C as directed in the manufacturer's instructions.

Place the gammon steaks in a small roasting tin that will fit on the high cooking rack. Coat the steaks with olive oil and cook it for 10 minutes. The steaks will be moist and tender, but if you prefer a dryer finish, cook for a further 5 minutes.

Bacon

- 4-6 bacon rashers. Serves 2

You do not need to preheat the Halogen Oven.

Arrange the rashers of bacon on the high cooking rack. Set the temperature to 250°C and cook for 10 minutes. For crispy bacon, cook for a further 2 or 3 minutes. Turn the bacon over half-way through the cooking time.

Roast Beef

• 3kg (1.5lb) joint of beef such as silverside which has a small amount of fat within the meat to keep it tender. Serves 4-6

Preheat the Halogen Oven to 175°C.
Place the beef joint in a roasting tin. Drizzle olive oil over the top. Cover and seal the meat in the tin with a layer of tinfoil. Start cooking in three 30-minute stages for a total of 90 minutes. After each stage turn the beef joint over. At the end of the cooking time allow the meat to stand for 15-20 minutes.

Fillet Steak

• 1 fillet steak about 1/2 inch thick per person
There is no need to preheat the Halogen Oven.

Place the fillet steak in a small roasting tin. Cover the steak with a few grinds of black pepper and a drizzle of olive oil. Cook on 200°C. As a general guide, 8-10 minutes for rare, 10-15 minutes for medium and approximately 20 minutes for a well done steak. The steak can be turned over half-way through the cooking time.

Chicken

• 1 chicken fillet of breast/thigh per person.
There is no need to preheat the Halogen Oven.

Any chicken portion with skin on can be roasted on the high cooking rack without the need for a casserole dish, and simply brushed with olive oil. Chicken without a skin will benefit from being placed in a small casserole dish with a small drizzle of olive oil which will help prevent the meat from drying out. A seasoning of salt and black pepper will help bring out the flavour. Cook on 200°C for 15-20 minutes or until the meat in the middle is white, piping hot, tender, and the juices run clear.

Vegetable Pasta Bake

A hearty meal full of goodness.

- Serves 2
- Use a low cooking rack
- You will need a casserole dish

Ingredients

- 200g (7oz) penne pasta
- 400g (14oz) tin of chopped tomatoes
- 1 medium head of broccoli chopped into florets
- 200g (7oz) tin kidney beans
- 1 yellow pepper, deseeded and sliced
- 150ml (5.5floz) double cream
- 100g (3.5oz) grated cheddar
- salt and black pepper

Method

Preheat the Halogen Oven to 200°C as directed in the manufacturer's instructions.

Boil the pasta as directed by the packet instructions. For the last 3 minutes add the chopped broccoli. Drain and put back into the pan.

Stir in all the remaining ingredients except for the cheese; season it with salt and black pepper and put into a casserole dish. Sprinkle the cheese on top and bake for 20 minutes or until golden brown. If the top is browning too quickly a sheet of tinfoil can be placed over the dish until the end of cooking time.

Quick and Easy Pasta

An incredibly easy and hassle-free supper.

- Serves 2
- Use a low cooking rack
- You will need a casserole dish

Ingredients

- 200g (7oz) penne pasta
- 2 medium free range eggs
- 2 tbsp double cream
- 100g (3.5oz) gruyere cheese, broken into chunks.
- salt and black pepper

Method

Preheat the Halogen Oven to 180°C as directed in the manufacturer's instructions.

Boil the pasta as directed by the packet instructions. Drain the pasta and put back into the pan. Allow to cool for a few minutes while you prepare the eggs.

Beat the eggs in a separate bowl, stir in the cream and add to the drained pasta. Don't stir too vigorously or the eggs could scramble; just gently fold them through.

Crumble the cheese all over the pasta, season with salt and black pepper and bake for 10-12 minutes until golden brown and the pasta on top is slightly crunchy.

Although this dish is deliciously simple as it is, you could add a chopped red chilli for heat and colour, or fried bacon cut into cubes . . . just experiment.

Roasted Peppers

A healthy and filling dinner.

- Serves 2
- Use a low cooking rack
- You will need a small casserole dish

Ingredients

- 1 pepper per person - chopped horizontally with the seeds scooped out
- 3 tbsp couscous
- 1 heaped tbsp cooked tinned lentils, drained
- juice of 1 lemon
- 1 clove of garlic, peeled and chopped
- 150ml (5floz) ready-made vegetable stock
- small handful of chopped parsley
- 25g (1oz) feta cheese, chopped into cubes
- salt and black pepper
- 2 tbsp olive oil

Method

Preheat the Halogen Oven to 200°C as directed in the manufacturer's instructions.

Season the peppers, drizzle with 1 tbsp of the oil, place in the casserole dish and roast for 15 minutes until soft and tender.

While the peppers are roasting, prepare the couscous stuffing. Pour the couscous into a bowl, add the lemon juice, garlic, and lentils. Pour the boiling stock over the couscous.

Cover with tinfoil and leave for 5 minutes while the couscous absorbs all the liquid.

Remove the foil and fluff up the couscous with a fork, ensuring the mixture is dry with no water still left to be absorbed, otherwise the mixture will be bland and stodgy. Stir through the remaining oil, chopped parsley and a few grinds of black pepper.

Tear off squares of tinfoil big enough to wrap each pepper and remove them to the foil. Spoon the mixture into each pepper, being careful not to overfill it, crumble over the feta, being as generous as you like, wrap up the peppers in the tinfoil and continue to roast for a further 15 minutes. When the 15 minutes is up, just open up the foil to expose the tops of the peppers and bake for a further 5 minutes to allow the feta to go golden brown and slightly crunchy. Serve with salad.

Top tip

Mixing in a chopped sprig of rosemary to the couscous mixture will add great flavour to the filling.

Broccoli and Mixed Cheese Quiche

A delicious way to use up leftover cheese!

- Serves 4-6
- Use a high cooking rack
- You will need a baking tray

Ingredients

- one 8 inch savoury flan case (can be bought ready-made)
- 115g (4oz) small broccoli florets
- 115g (4oz) mixed cheese, grated
- pinch of grated nutmeg
- black pepper
- 250ml (18 fl oz) double or whipping cream
- 2 eggs, beaten

Method

Preheat the Halogen Oven to 180°C as directed in the manufacturer's instructions.

Boil the broccoli in a small pan of boiling water until it is just soft.

Sprinkle the cheese into the flan case.

Arrange the cooked broccoli on top of the cheese.

Beat the two eggs, cream, nutmeg and pepper in a bowl and gently pour over the cheese and broccoli.

Cook at 180°C for 15 minutes or until the top of the quiche is golden.

Roast Chicken Dinner

A one-pot solution to a Sunday favourite.

- Serves 2
- Use a low cooking rack

Ingredients

- small or medium chicken (1.5 -2kg/ 3.3lb-4.4lb)
- 1 or 2 small onions chopped into quarters
- 4tbls olive oil
- 4 carrots chopped into chunky sticks
- 2 parsnips chopped into chunky sticks
- 4 small potatoes cut into quarters

Method

Preheat the Halogen Oven to 175°C as directed in the manufacturer's instructions.

In a bowl, toss all the vegetables in olive oil, ensuring they are all coated in the oil.

Place the chicken on the low cooking rack and arrange all the vegetables around it. Coat the chicken in a little more oil; there will be no need to baste the chicken later.

Leave to cook for 1 1/2 hours. Check the chicken is cooked by pushing a skewer through the middle to see if the juice runs clear.

Top tip
Adding a few drops of soy sauce over the chicken skin helps get a roasted, brown colouring.

Mediterranean Chicken

Big flavours for little effort.

- Serves 2
- Use a low cooking rack
- You will need a casserole dish

Ingredients

- 4 medium sized chicken thighs
- handful of cherry tomatoes
- handful of new potatoes, chopped in half.
- handful of olives
- salt and black pepper
- approximately 4tbls olive oil

Method

Preheat the Halogen Oven to 180°C as directed in the manufacturer's instructions.

Place the potatoes, tomatoes and olives in the casserole dish, then place the chicken thighs on top. (You could add a few torn basil leaves for extra flavour).

Season with salt and black pepper and a small drizzle of olive oil. Bake for 1 hour, turning the chicken half-way through.

When the chicken is cooked, the meat will come away from the bone with little effort and the skin will be beautifully crisp and sticky.

Chicken Escalopes

Chicken in a crispy breadcrumb coating.

• Serves 2 • Use a low cooking rack
• You will need a casserole dish

Ingredients

• 2 chicken breast fillets
• 2 tbsp plain flour
• 1 egg, beaten
• 4 tbsp breadcrumbs
• 2 tomatoes, roughly chopped
• 1 clove garlic
• a few basil leaves, chopped
• 2 tbsp olive oil
• 100g (3.5oz) mozzarella
• salt and black pepper

Method

Preheat the oven to 200°C as directed in the manufacturer's instructions.

Lay the fillets on a chopping board and cut through the middle horizontally, without going all the way through. Fold back the top layer to open out the fillet. Doing this will help it cook much more quickly.

Arrange three small plates, one with flour, one with the beaten egg and one with breadcrumbs. Season the flour, then coat the chicken, ensuring an even coverage; dust off any excess. Dip the fillet into the egg, followed by the breadcrumbs and coat evenly on each side. Repeat for the other chicken fillet.

Place the chicken in the casserole dish and cook in the oven for 10 minutes while you prepare the sauce. Mix the tomato, basil, garlic and 1 tbsp of the oil. Season with salt and black pepper and mix. Turn the chicken fillets over in the oven and spoon the tomato mixture on top. Tear up the mozzarella over each chicken fillet, add the remainder of the oil, and continue to bake for a further 15 minutes or until golden brown and the cheese is slightly bubbling.

LONICERA

Pork Steaks with Honey-Glazed Apple Slices

A simple idea that tastes as good as it looks.

- Serves 2
- Use a low cooking rack

Ingredients

- 2 pork steaks
- 2 apples, finely sliced
- runny honey (the bottle type)

Method

Preheat the Halogen Oven to 200°C as directed in the manufacturer's instructions.

Place the two pork steaks on the high cooking rack and set the timer for 20 minutes. Begin cooking.

After ten minutes turn the steaks over and cover with the apple slices. Drizzle honey over the apple slices.

Continue cooking for the remaining ten minutes.

Marinated Pork Chops

For maximum flavour, prepare a day in advance.

- Serves 2
- Use a high cooking rack
- You will need a casserole dish

Ingredients

- 2 pork chops
- 2 cloves garlic, unpeeled and lightly crushed
- 2 tbsp sesame oil
- 1-2 fresh red chillies, de-seeded and chopped
- 1 tbsp soy sauce
- Salt and black pepper

Method

Put all the ingredients into a dish. Cover with foil and leave to marinate in the fridge overnight, or a minimum of 45 minutes.

When you are ready to cook your pork chops, preheat the oven to 180°C.

Remove the marinated mixture from the fridge and remove the foil. Cook in the preheated oven for 15 minutes, turning the meat over half-way through. Great served with chips, mash, rice or salad.

Top tip
Adding a little fresh rosemary and thyme to the marinade will really enhance the flavour, smell and appearance of your dish.

Beef Casserole

With or without the mashed potato topping, this recipe is a s-mash hit!

- Serves 2
- Use a low cooking rack
- You will need a casserole dish

Ingredients

- 400g (14oz) braising steak
- 2 large carrots
- 1 leek
- 1 butternut squash
- 300g (11oz) new potatoes
- 1 medium onion
- salt and black pepper
- 400ml (14floz) beef stock
- 150ml (5.5floz) red wine (optional)

Method

Preheat the Halogen Oven to 200°C as directed in the manufacturer's instructions.

Chop the beef and vegetables into 2-3cm (1 inch) chunks and season generously with salt and black pepper; then place in the casserole dish and cook for several minutes to lightly brown the ingredients. If using wine add it now.

Cook through for 4-5 minutes, or until the wine has mostly evaporated.

Add the stock to the casserole, ensuring all the vegetables and meat are covered.

Cook for 60 minutes, stirring every 10 minutes.

The casserole is ready to eat when the vegetables and the meat are tender. Season and serve.

Why not add a mashed potato topping to your casserole?

Ingredients

- 3-4 medium Maris Piper potatoes
- salt and black pepper
- 25g (1oz) salted butter
- 100g (3.5oz) grated cheddar
- 1 large egg yolk

Method

While the casserole is cooking, cut the potatoes into bite-sized chunks and add to a pan of salted boiling water.

Boil for 10-15 minutes or until the potatoes are tender. The potatoes are ready when a knife passes through them smoothly.

Drain the potatoes and put them back into the pan.

Add the butter and mash the potato until smooth. Add 3/4 of the cheese, the egg yolk, a pinch of salt and black pepper, and stir through.

Approximately 15 minutes before the end of cooking time, remove the dish and spread the potato mixture on top. Add the remaining cheese on top, fluff with a fork and bake for 10-15 minutes until golden brown.

Roast Beef with Roasted Vegetables

This method takes the stress out of getting all the vegetables ready at the same time.

- Serves 2-3
- Use the low cooking rack

Ingredients

- 3/4kg (1.5lb) beef joint such as silverside
- 3-4 carrots
- 3-4 potatoes
- 1 parsnip
- 1 head of broccoli
- 1 onion or 4 shallots
- a few drops of soy sauce (optional)

Method

Preheat the Halogen Oven to 200°C as directed in the manufacturer's instructions.

Brown each side of the beef in a frying pan in a small amount of oil. If a hob isn't available put the beef straight into a roasting tin and cover with a lid of tinfoil. Place the beef on the low cooking rack and cook for 30 minutes.

Cut all the vegetables into similar sized pieces. Cut the carrots and parsnips lengthways, then again into 4cm (2 inch) pieces.

The onion can be cut into 4 pieces and the shallots can be either left whole or cut in two.

Put the vegetables, except the broccoli, into a bowl. Cover with 3 tbsp of olive oil and sprinkle a few drops of soy sauce over them. Mix well, so that the vegetables are covered in the dressing.

After the first 30 minutes, place the vegetables into the bottom of the Halogen Oven around the outside of the low cooking rack. Turn the meat over in its roasting tin, replace the foil and cook for a further 30 minutes.

Meanwhile, cut the broccoli into small florets and wrap in tinfoil, adding 2 tbsp of water; add this tinfoil parcel to the oven. Stir the vegetables. Turn and baste the meat once more. Cook for a final 30 minutes, then remove the meat dish. Keep the meat covered but allow it to 'rest' for about 15 minutes before carving.

Test the vegetables with a fork to see if they are cooked. If they are, turn the temperature down to 100C to keep them warm. While the meat is resting, you will have time to make gravy and even pop a few ready-made Yorkshire puddings into the oven. They will only take 2/3 minutes to heat through.

Homemade Burgers

Easier than you may think!

- Makes 4 burgers
- Use a low cooking rack
- You will need a baking tray

Ingredients

- 500g (18oz) beef mince
- 1 onion, finely chopped
- pinch of cumin and coriander (optional)
- 2 heaped tsp of Dijon mustard
- 1 tbsp tomato ketchup
- 1 medium egg
- 5 tbsp breadcrumbs
- salt and black pepper

Method

Preheat the oven to 200°C as directed in the manufacturer's instructions.

Put all the ingredients into a large bowl and mix with your hands until it's all incorporated. Add more breadcrumbs if it's too sticky and wet: you want a nice smooth patty. If you are not using the mixture straightaway it can be covered in tinfoil and left in the fridge for up to two days.

Mould and roll the mixture into 4 round patties and place on a baking tray on the low cooking rack. Bake in the oven for 20 minutes, carefully turning over half-way through.

If you want to check that they're done, cut one in half to ensure the meat is no longer pink, but has turned brown.

Serve in toasted burger buns with salad.

Tartiflette

A creamy and indulgent French dish.

- Serves 2 • Use a low cooking rack
- You will need a casserole dish

Ingredients

- 3 medium Maris Piper potatoes
- 2 thick rashes of bacon
- 1 medium onion
- 60g (2oz) soft, creamy cheese such as Reblochon cut into cubes
- 200ml (7 fl oz) double cream
- 100ml (3.5floz) milk
- Salt and black pepper
- 2 tbsp bread crumbs (optional)
- 1 tbsp of grated Parmesan (or Cheddar)

Method

Preheat the Halogen Oven to 200°C as directed in the manufacturer's instructions. Put the casserole dish in the oven to warm.

Peel and finely slice the potatoes. Add to a pan of boiling salted water for 4-5 minutes until slightly tender. Drain, set aside and keep warm.

Meanwhile, cut the bacon into cubes and place in the hot casserole dish with a drizzle of olive oil. Cook for 2-3 minutes. Peel, roughly chop and add the onion. Stir.

When the onion is soft but not browned and the bacon is becoming crisp, add all the potatoes and arrange them on top. Cook for a further 5 minutes to add a little colour.

Add the cheese to the dish and season all over. Mix the milk and cream and pour over, then grate over the Parmesan. Bake for 60 minutes adding the breadcrumbs on top for the last 5 minutes if you're using them. If it's cooking too quickly on top, add a square of tinfoil.

Top tip
Take a broccoli head
and cut into small florets.
Wrap in tinfoil adding a tbsp
of water. Place in the bottom
of the oven and cook at the
same time as the fish.

Baked Cod

Perfect, flaky cod every time.

- Serves 2 • Use a high cooking rack
- You will need a baking tray

Ingredients

- 2 cod steaks
- 1 tomato or 2 tbsp chopped sundried tomatoes
- Small packet of lemon and thyme stuffing
- 115g (4oz) grated cheese (Cheddar, Edam or Red Leicester work well)

Method

Preheat the Halogen Oven to 200°C as directed in the manufacturer's instructions.

Place the cod steaks on a small baking tray lined with tinfoil. Cover the fish in thin slices of tomato. Sprinkle the dry stuffing mix over the top of the fish, followed by the cheese.

Bake for 15 minutes on the high cooking rack until the fish breaks into flakes.

Or why not try . . .

Salmon with Parsley Butter

Preheat the Halogen Oven to 200°C as directed in the manufacturer's instructions.

Take 2 salmon fillets. Mix freshly chopped parsley into a tbsp of softened butter. Spread the butter over the fillets, place them into a small ovenproof dish and cook on the high cooking rack, for 10 minutes.

Salmon with Ratatouille

A complete meal, full of colour and flavour.

- Serves 2
- Use a low cooking rack
- You will need a small casserole dish

Ingredients

- 2 salmon fillets
- 1 medium red onion, peeled and chopped
- 1 courgette, diced
- 1 aubergine, deseeded and diced
- 1 red pepper, deseeded and diced.
- 400g (14oz) tin of chopped tomatoes
- juice of 1 lemon
- 1 glass white wine
- pinch of sugar
- salt and black pepper
- 4 tbsp olive oil
- handful of fresh basil leaves (optional)

Method

Preheat the Halogen Oven to 200°C as directed in the manufacturer's instructions.

Pour half the oil into the casserole dish and place in the oven while you prepare the vegetables. Season the salmon with salt and black pepper and put in the fridge.

Add the onion to the casserole dish and stir to coat in the oil; cook for 4-5 minutes. Add the courgette and aubergine along with the remaining oil and stir well. Cook for a further 8 minutes, stirring now and then until the vegetables are becoming tender. Add the pepper, tomatoes, sugar, lemon juice, wine and basil leaves if you're using them and stir. Cook for approximately 25 minutes, stirring occasionally until the sauce has thickened and the vegetables are soft.

Remove the seasoned salmon from the fridge and place on top of the sauce, skin side up. Cook for a further 8 minutes, turning the salmon over half-way through.

Something Tasty On Toast

If you need a snack in a hurry, a topping on toast is ideal. This method is easier than using a grill and much less likely to burn!

• Serves 1-2 • Use a high cooking rack

Ingredients

• 2 slices of bread • 2oz grated cheese (Cheddar) • 1 sliced tomato

Method

There is no need to preheat the Halogen Oven for this recipe.

Put 2 slices of bread on the high cooking rack. Cover with tomato, then the grated cheese. Cook for 5 minutes on 200°C.

Here are a few more ideas, but there really is no limit:

- Try different cheese combinations such as Edam and Cheshire, Dolchelatte and Cheddar, Stilton and Cheddar
- Sliced mushrooms, with tomato.
- Slices of pepperoni, tomatoes and cheese.
- Tapenade and goats' cheese.
- Thinly chopped ham, tomatoes and grated cheese.
- Tinned baked beans. No need to pre-heat the beans in a pan. Cook the bread slices for 2 minutes, then spoon the beans onto the toast and cook for a further 3 minutes.
- Tinned chilli con carne, slices of fresh tomato topped with grated cheese. Heat the bread for 1 min, spread with the chilli con carne, cook for 2 minutes. Add the tomatoes and cheese. Cook for 2 minutes.
- Grated onion and cheese.

Welsh Rarebit

The perfect tasty topping for toast.

- Makes enough to cover 6 slices of toast
- Use a high cooking rack

Ingredients

- 25g (1oz) butter
- 25g (1oz) plain flour
- 150ml (5fl oz) milk or 300ml (10fl oz) if not using beer
- 150ml (5fl oz) beer, such as brown ale (optional)
- 175g (6oz) grated cheese
- 2 egg yolks, beaten
- 3-4 drops Worcester sauce
- 1/4 tsp dry English mustard
- salt and black pepper

Method

There is no need to preheat the Halogen Oven for this recipe.

Melt the butter on a low heat, add the flour and mustard and stir the mixture well. Add all the liquid very gradually, stirring all the time. The mixture will thicken.

Now add the beaten egg yolks and the cheese and blend to a smooth, thick mixture.

Spoon generous amounts of the mixture onto thick bread and cook on the high cooking rack for 4-5 minutes on 250°C.

You can toast one side of the bread first for a crunchier result by placing slices of bread on the high cooking rack for 2 minutes, then turn the bread over before adding the Welsh Rarebit mixture.

Top tip
The Rarebit mixture can be frozen and stored for 2-3 months.

Top tip

Mix the milk and the cream in a saucepan and heat gently to a gradual boil before mixing with the potatoes. Adding some chopped herbs and garlic at this stage will add an extra dimension to the overall flavour.

Potato Dauphinoise

A great accompanying dish for meat, fish or vegetables.

- Serves 4
- Use a low cooking rack
- You will need a casserole dish

Ingredients

- 5 medium Maris Piper potatoes
- 350ml (12floz) cream
- 350ml (12floz) milk
- 80g (3oz) Gruyére cheese (Cheddar will also work)
- salt and black pepper

Method

Preheat the Halogen Oven to 200°C as directed in the manufacturer's instructions.

Peel and finely slice the potatoes. Mix the milk and cream together.

Layer half the potatoes in a casserole dish, cover with half the milk and cream mixture, sprinkle over half the cheese, and season with salt and black pepper. Repeat this process with the remaining ingredients.

Bake for 60 minutes until golden brown and the potatoes are nice and tender and the milk and cream mixture has thickened.

Olive Bread

Great for parties or as a tasty snack.

- Serves 4-6
- Use a low cooking rack
- You will need a baking tray

Ingredients

- 500g (18oz) strong white plain flour; the better the quality, the better the flavour
- 7g sachet dried yeast
- 1tsp salt
- 325ml (11floz) lukewarm water
- 2 tbsp extra virgin olive oil

For the Olive Spread

- 150g (5.5oz) pitted black olives
- 1 tbsp olive oil
- black pepper to season
- 1 heaped tsp paprika (optional)
- 2 cloves of garlic (optional)
- a few basil leaves (optional)

Method

Sieve the flour and salt into a large bowl, add the dried yeast and mix, then make a well in the centre. Mix the water and olive oil, and pour a little into the well, mixing with a fork. When the mixture becomes dry, add a little more water and continue until the water has gone.

Lightly flour a work surface and turn the mixture out onto it. Knead the mixture until you have a soft and springy dough, a minimum of 5 minutes; however, there is no set method; twist, pull, push and squeeze! Place the dough in a large bowl, cover with cling film and leave in a warm place for 2 hours and until it has doubled in size.

After 2 hours, lightly knead the dough again to squeeze out excess air. Wrap in cling film and leave it in the fridge while you prepare the olive mixture.

Preheat the Halogen Oven to 200°C as directed in the manufacturer's instructions.

Place all the ingredients in a bowl, crushing and mixing with a fork until you have a rough spread. Set aside. Roll out the dough to a thickness of about 1cm (1/2 inch) and into a long rectangular shape. Spread the olive mixture on top of the dough, going right up to the edges.

Starting from the edge nearest to you, gently roll up the dough, creating a Swiss roll effect. Trim a few centimetres off each edge and then cut into slices of approximately 5-6 cm (2 inches) in thickness. You should have about 5 slices. Place on a baking tray. Season with pepper and bake for 15 minutes until golden brown.

Top tip
For extra crispiness coat the potatoes in semolina flour between parboiling and putting them in the oven.

Roast Potatoes

The perfect accompaniment to any roast dinner.

• Serves 4

Ingredients

• 4 large potatoes
• vegetable oil
• 1 tbsp soy sauce

Method

Preheat the Halogen Oven to 200°C as directed in the manufacturer's instructions.

Peel the potatoes and cut them into even-sized pieces. Parboil the potatoes, drain them and allow them to cool.

Pour enough oil to cover the bottom of the oven and re-heat for another 5 minutes.

Add the potatoes and sprinkle with soy sauce. Cook the potatoes for approximately 1 hour or until the potatoes are golden brown.

Cheesy Biscuits

Moreish nibbles, great with a glass of wine!

- Makes approximately 16 biscuits
- Use a high cooking rack
- You will need a baking tray

Ingredients

- 115g (4oz) whole wheat flour
- 115g (4oz) butter
- 1/2 tsp salt
- 1/4 tsp black pepper
- pinch cayenne pepper or English mustard powder
- 115g (4oz) grated Cheddar cheese
- 115g (4oz) grated Parmesan cheese

Method

Preheat the Halogen Oven to 175°C as directed in the manufacturer's instructions.

Rub the butter into the flour and add the salt, black pepper and either the cayenne pepper or English mustard powder.

Add the cheeses and mix well to make a dough (a food processor can be used at this stage).

Shape the dough into a thick roll, about 10 inches long. Place the roll on a tray and pop into the freezer for 20 minutes to make the dough firm.

After 20 minutes, take the dough out of the freezer and cut into thin, even slices to make the biscuits.

Place on a greased or lined baking tray and bake for 8-10 minutes. You will need to cook the biscuits in two batches. Let the biscuits cool for 10 minutes to become firm.

Apple and Blackberry Bake

Delicious served with custard or ice-cream.

- Serves 6
- Use a low cooking rack
- You will need an oven-proof dish

Ingredients

- 6 apples, peeled and sliced
- 140g (5oz) blackberries
- 60g (2oz) caster sugar

For the Topping:

- 115g (4oz) self-raising flour
- 1 tsp cinnamon
- 60g (2oz) softened butter
- 60g (2oz) caster sugar
- 1 egg beaten
- 3 tbsp of milk

Method

Preheat the Halogen Oven to 200°C as directed in the manufacturer's instructions.

Soften the apple slices in a pan with the caster sugar and a tbsp of water; keep on a low heat so they don't burn.

While the apples are softening, prepare the topping by mixing all the ingredients together to form a thick batter. This stage can be achieved using a food processor or a large mixing bowl and some vigorous stirring.

Place the softened apples in the oven-proof dish and sprinkle with the blackberries. Drop spoonfuls of the batter mix over the fruit.

Bake for 15-20 minutes or until the top is golden brown and firm to touch.

Cupcakes

Fluffy, golden and great with a cup of tea!

- Makes approximately 12 cupcakes
- Use a low cooking rack
- You will need a cupcake tray that will fit into the Halogen Oven.

Ingredients

- 110g (4oz) self-raising flour, sifted
- 110g (4oz) caster sugar, sifted
- 110g (4oz) unsalted butter or margarine
- 2 large, free range eggs
- 1tsp vanilla extract
- 1tsp baking powder
- icing and decorations; these can be bought ready-made

Method

Preheat the Halogen Oven to 200°C as directed in the manufacturer's instructions. Put the cupcake cases into the cupcake tray.

Put the sugar and the fat into a large bowl, then, using either a hand whisk or an electric whisk, beat the mixture until smooth.

Add half the flour and beat the mixture well before adding one egg, beating the mixture until smooth. Repeat this process with the remaining flour and egg. Add the baking powder and the vanilla extract. Beat the mixture to a smooth consistency.

Spoon the mixture into the cases using about 2-3 tsp of the mixture for each case.

Bake for 12 minutes. The cupcakes are ready when they are firm but slightly bouncy to the touch, or when a skewer is placed into the middle of the cake and it comes out clean.

Afternoon Tea Scones

An English classic that is easy in a Halogen Oven

- Makes approximately 8-10 scones
- Use a high cooking rack
- You will need a baking tray

Ingredients

- 225g (8oz) self-raising flour
- 1/2 tsp salt
- 1 tsp baking powder
- 60g (2oz) butter
- 1/4 pint milk (or half milk and half sour cream)
- 1 tbsp caster sugar
- 1 beaten egg to glaze (optional)

Method

Preheat the Halogen Oven to 200°C as directed in the manufacturer's instructions. Grease the baking tray.

Rub the butter into the flour, salt and baking powder to make a crumbly mixture which resembles breadcrumbs.

Add the milk gradually until the mixture starts to stick together into one big ball.

Shape and pat it into a 1/2 inch slab, using your hands not a rolling pin, in order to keep the dough light.

Cut 8-10 scones out of the mixture with a round pastry cutter, about 2 inches in diameter.

Place the scones on the pre-greased baking tray and glaze with beaten egg.
Place the tray on the high cooking rack and cook for 10 minutes.

Remove the scones and allow to cool for 10 minutes before cutting in two and serving with cream and jam.

Mincemeat and Apple Slice

This easy recipe can be eaten hot with cream or cold the next day as a lunch-time pudding.

- Serves 6
- Use a low cooking rack
- You will need a baking tray

Ingredients

- 175g (6oz) butter
- 75g (2.5oz) caster sugar
- 150g (5.5oz) plain flour
- 1tsp baking powder
- 2 egg yolks

For the Topping

- 400g (14oz) mincemeat
- 3 apples, sliced
- 50g (1.75oz) melted butter
- 3tbsp caster sugar

Method for the Base

Preheat the Halogen Oven to 200°C as directed in the manufacturer's instructions.

In either a bowl or a food processor, mix the butter, sugar, flour and baking powder and eggs until the mixture sticks together.

Press the mixture flat into a cake tin and bake for 10 minutes. Remove to a work-surface.

Method for the Topping

Spread the mincemeat over the cooked base. This is made easier if you warm the mincemeat for a few minutes first in your Halogen Oven. Lay the apple slices over the top of the mincemeat, overlapping the slices slightly.

Drizzle the melted butter over the apple and sprinkle with the sugar before baking for a further 10 minutes.

Conversion Charts

Oven Temperatures

Temperatures are guidelines only. Most food will be cooked between 175°C and 200°C. The standard highest setting of 250°C will be used to grill food in your Halogen Oven.

°C	°F
125	257
150	302
175	347
200	392
225	437
250	482

Liquid Measures

Metric	Imperial
30ml	1 fl oz
60ml	2 fl oz
100ml	3 fl oz
125ml	4 fl oz
150ml	5 fl oz
190ml	6 fl oz
250ml	8 fl oz
300ml	10 fl oz
500ml	16 fl oz

Dry Measures

Metric	Imperial
30g	1oz
60g	2oz
125g	4oz
185g	6oz
250g	8oz
315g	10oz
375g	12oz
400g	14oz
500g	16oz